THE IRISH SPIRIT

IRISH PROVERBS
LAURENCE FLANAGAN

IRISH SUPERSTITIONS
BY DÁITHÍ Ó HÓGÁIN

IRISH FAIRY TALES
BY PADRAIC O'FARRELL

GRAMERCY BOOKS
New York

This book was originally published in separate volumes under the titles:

Irish Fairy Tales, copyright © 1977 by Padraic O'Farrell

Irish Superstitions, copyright © 1995 by Dáithí Ó hÓgáin

Irish Proverbs, copyright © 1995 by Laurence Flanagan

This 1999 edition is published by Gramercy Books™, an imprint of Random House Value Publishing, Inc., 201 East 50th Street, New York, N.Y. 10022, by arrangement with Gill & Macmillan Ltd.

Gramercy Books™ and colophon are trademarks of Random House Value Publishing, Inc.

Random House
New York • Toronto • London • Sydney • Auckland
http://www.randomhouse.com/

Printed in the United States of America

A CIP catalog record for this book is available from the Library of Congress.

ISBN 0-517-20168-2

8 7 6 5 4 3 2 1

IRISH PROVERBS

Compiled by
LAURENCE FLANAGAN

For FERGAL TOBIN

Contents

Preface

'Every civilised language possesses a large store of proverbs, the accumulated gatherings of the wit and homely wisdom of many generations. Numbers of these are identical, or nearly so, in all countries, seeming, as it were, to be citizens of the world.' This was said in 1858 by Robert MacAdam in his introduction to a collection of Ulster proverbs. The truth of it will be seen in the following pages. One of the inevitabilities of compiling lists of proverbs is that plagiarism is implicit in it — or rather, since several sources are used, 'research'. The practice of compiling lists of Irish proverbs has a long ancestry, going back to such ancient compilations as 'Tecosca Cormaic' [Teagasc Chormaic], ascribed to the mythical Cormac mac Airt. Since those early efforts many people have assiduously collected proverbs throughout the country, thereby preserving them for us and posterity. The basis of the present selection is a list that appeared in *The College Irish Grammar* by Rev. Ulick Bourke, who was intent on producing a more definitive collection, which unfortunately never materialised. Items from this source are indicated by [B]. To this are added items from the MacAdam collection, indicated by [MA], items from a collection by Henry Morris, indicated by [M], and a collection compiled in the eighteenth century by Micheál Ó Longáin, indicated by [OL]. A number of proverbs gleaned from Irish literature listed by T. F. O'Rahilly are added; these are indicated by [OR]. The Irish versions are those given by the original compilers, without any alteration or modernisation, while the English renderings are also those put upon them by the compilers.

Many appear to be duplications but in fact are slightly
variant forms, perhaps from different parts of the country.
One not included in the body of this selection is almost
an Irish Ten Commandments and seems a fitting end to
this preface.

Ná bí cainteach a d-tigh an óil,
Ná cuir anfhios air sheanóir,
Ná h-abair nach n-déantar cóir,
Ná h-ob agus na h-iarr onóir,
Ná bí cruaidh agus ná bí bog,
Ná tréig do charaid air a chuid,
Ná bí mí-mhodhamhail, ná déan troid,
A's ná h-ob í ma's éigin duit.

Do not be talkative in a drinking-house,
Do not impute ignorance to an elder,
Do not say justice is not done,
Do not refuse and do not seek honour,
Do not be hard and do not be liberal,
Do not forsake a friend on account of his means,
Do not be impolite; and do not offer fight,
Yet decline it not, if necessary. [B]

Advice

1   Comhairle charaid gan a h-íarraidh, chan fhuair si
    a ríamh an meas budh chóir di.
    A friend's advice not asked for was never valued
    as it deserved. [MA]

2   Is olc nach ngabhaidh comhairle, acht is míle measa
    a ghabhas gach uile chomhairle.
    He is bad that will not take advice, but he is a thousand
    times worse who takes every advice. [MA]

3   An té ná gabhann cómhairle gabhadh sé cómhrac.
    Let him who will not have advice have conflict. [OL]

4   Minic bhí duine 'na dhroch-chómhairlidhe dho féin
    agus 'na chómhairlidhe mhaith do dhuine eile.
    A man is often a bad adviser to himself and a good
    adviser to another. [OL]

Appetite

5   Maith an mustárd an sliabh.
    The mountain is a good mustard. [OL]

6   Is maith a t-annlann an t-ocras.
    Hunger is the best sauce. [OL]

Application

7   Ní fhaghann cos 'na comhnaidh aon nídh.
    The foot at rest meets nothing. [B]

8   Ma bhris tu an cnámh, char dhiúghail tu an smior.
    Though you have broken the bone you have not sucked
    out the marrow. [MA]

9   Is fearr rith maith ná seasamh fada.
     A good run is better than a long stand. [MA]

10   Budh chóir an dán a dheanadh go maith air tús, mur
     is iomad fear millte a thig air.
     *A poem ought to be well made at first, for there is many a
     one to spoil it afterwards.* [MA]

11   Is namhuid an cheird gan a foghluim í.
     A trade not (properly) learned is an enemy. [MA]

12   'Si leith na ceirde an úirleais.
     The tools are the half of the trade. [MA]

13   Is fearr díomhaineach ná ag obair a n-asgaidh.
     Better be idle than working for nothing. [MA]

14   Buail an t-iarann fad a's ta se teith.
     Strike while the iron is hot. [MA]

15   Cha ghabhann dorn druidte seabhac.
     A shut fist will not catch a hawk. [MA]

16   Chan fhaghthar saill gan saothar.
     Fat is not to be had without labour. [MA]

17   Sé an t-éun maidne a gheabhas a phéideog.
     It is the morning bird that catches the worm. [MA]

18   Is trian de'n obair, tús a chur.
     Making a beginning is the one-third of the work. [MA]

19   Dean sin mur a bheidheadh teine air do chraicionn.
     Do it as if there were fire on your skin. [MA]

20   An té is luaithe lamh, bíodh aige an gadhar bán 's
     a fiadh.
     *He that has the quickest hand, let him have the white
     hound and the deer.* [MA]

21 Is fearr éirigh moch ná suidhe mall.
Early rising is better than sitting up late. [MA]

22 Faghann iarraidh iarraidh eile.
The seeking for one thing will find another. [MA]

23 Ni'l ó mheud an phráinn nach lughaide na
gnothuidhe.
The greater the hurry the less the work. [MA]

24 Trom an rud an leisge.
Laziness is a load. [OL]

25 Cuir luath is buin luath.
Early sow, early mow. [OL]

26 As an obair do fachtar an fhoghluim.
Learning comes through work. [OL]

27 Gnáthamh na hoibre an t-eólas.
Knowledge comes through practice. [OL]

28 Gibé olc maith an ealadha, is taithighe néann
máighistreacht.
*Be one's trade good or bad, it is experience that makes one
an adept at it.* [OL]

29 I gcosaibh na con do bhíonn a cuid.
A greyhound finds its food with its feet. [OL]

30 Ní fhaghann cos 'na comhnaidhe dada.
A foot that stirs not gets nothing. [OL]

Beauty

31 Ailneacht mná ionraice guidheann cuntus cruaidh.
The beauty of a chaste woman excites hard dispute. [B]

29 I gcosaibh na con do bhíonn a cuid.
A greyhound finds its food with its feet. [OL]

32 Bidh borb faoi sgéimh.
A fierce person is often in beauty's dress. [B]

33 Is minic a bhí grána geanamhail, agus
dathamhail dona.
Often was ugly amiable and pretty sulky. [B]

34 Leis a mhéin a bhréagtar ach uile nidh, acht béidh an
sgiamh ag an té ar geineadh dó í.
*Beauty is the possession of him to whom it is born, but it is
manner that captivates every one.* [M]

35 Biann duilleabhar áluinn a's toradh searbh air chrann
na sgéimhe.
The tree of beauty has handsome foliage and bitter fruit.
[MA]

36 Minic bhí gránna greannmhar is dathamail donaoi.
Often was ugly amiable and handsome unfortunate. [OL]

37 Ní hí an bhreághthacht do chuireann an crocán
a' fiuchadh.
Beauty will not make the pot boil. [OL]

Begging

38 Is fearr mathair phócáin ná athair seistrigh.
A begging mother is better than a ploughing father. [MA]

39 Ní bhfaghann sír-iarraidh ach sír-eiteach.
Constant begging only meets with constant refusal. [OL]

Bribery

40 Sgoilteann an bhreab an chloch.
Bribery can split a stone. [OL]

41   Ní háil liom fear breibe.
      I like not a man who is bribed. [OL]

Charity

42   Dean taise le truaighe, a's gruaim le namhuid.
      Have a kind look for misery, but a frown for an enemy.
      [MA]

43   Ní bhfachtar maith le mugha agus fachtar clú le déirc.
      No good is got by wasting, but a good name is got by
      alms-giving. [OL]

Cleanliness

44   Is don ghlóire an ghluine.
      Cleanliness is part of glory. [OL]

Co-operation

45   Beirbh birín dam is beireód birín duit.
      Cook a little spit for me and I'll cook one for you. [OL]

46   Bíonn an rath i mbun na ronna.
      There is luck in sharing a thing. [OL]

Cures

47   Dóchar liaigh gach anró.
      Hope, the physician of all misery. [B]

48   Otracht sodh an leaghaidh.
      Distemper is the physician's luck. [B]

49 An nidh nach féadar a léigheas, is éigin 'fhulaing.
What cannot be cured must be endured. [MA]

50 An luibh ná fachtar fhóireann, adeir siad.
The herb that is not got is the one that cures, they say.
[OL]

51 Ar an rud nach féadfar do leigheas isí an fhoighde
is fearr.
For what cannot be cured patience is the best remedy. [OL]

52 Ni'l brigh 'san luibh nach bh-faghthar a n-ám.
There is no virtue in the herb that is not got in time. [MA]

Death

53 Is iomdha lá 'sa g-cill orainn.
Many a day shall we rest in the clay. [B]

54 Liagh gach boicht bás.
Death is every poor man's physician. [B]

55 Níor thug an bás, spás do dhuine air bith a riamh.
*Death, when its hour arrives, never granted any
one a respite.* [B]

56 Sona ádhluic fliuc.
A wet burying is lucky. [B]

57 Níor bhlas sé an biadh nach mblasfaidh an bás.
He has not tasted food who will not taste death. [M]

58 Is iomdha cor ag an bhás le baint as an duine.
Death has many ways of taking a turn out of a person.
[M]

59 Tá na daoine greannmhara uilig sa' tsiorruidheacht.
The pleasant humorous people are all in eternity. [M]

60 Is ionann 's a cás, a t-éug 's a bás.
To die and to lose one's life are much the same. [MA]

61 Biann dúil le béul fairge, acht cha bhiann le
béul uaighe.
There is hope from the mouth of the sea, but not from the
mouth of the grave. [MA]

62 Cha d-tig an bás gan adhbhar.
Death does not come without a reason. [MA]

63 Cabhair an bhochtáin, béul na h-uaighe.
The poor man's relief is the mouth of the grave. [MA]

64 Ní thig éag gan adhbhar.
Death does not come without a cause. [OL]

65 Dearbhráthair don bhás an codladh.
Sleep is brother to death. [OL]

66 Fearr súil le glas ná súil le huaigh.
Better expectation of release from imprisonment than of
release from the grave. [OL]

Debt

67 Cuntas glan fhagas cáirde buidheach
A charas Criosd, cuir a nall an fheóirlin.
Clear accounts leave friends thankful;
So, gossip, hand me over the farthing. [MA]

68 Ní dhíolann dearmhad fiacha.
Forgetting a debt does not pay it. [OL]

69 Is gnáth sealbh ar gach síoriasacht.
A long-continued loan usually confers ownership. [OR]

70   Is fiach ma gelltar.
A promise is a debt. [OR]

71   Is fochen aged fhécheman.
Welcome is a debtor's face. [OR]

Discretion

72   An rud nach bh-fághtar sé fhóireas.
What cannot be had is just what suits. [B]

73   Deacair dreim leis an mhuir mhór.
Hard to contend with the wide ocean. [B]

74   Dearc sul léim a tabhart.
Look before giving a leap. [B]

75   Gach am ní h-eagnach saoi.
At all times a sage is not wise. [B]

76   Má's fada lá tig oidhche.
If the day is long, night comes (at last). [B]

77   Moladh gach aon an t-áth mar do gheabhfaidh.
Let each man praise the ford as he finds it. [B]

78   Ná tabhair do bhreith air an g-céad sgeul,
Go m-beiridh an taobh eile ort.
Do not give your judgement on (hearing) the first story,
Until the other side is brought before you. [B]

79   Ni'l fios aig duine cia is feárr — an luas 'na 'n mhoill.
One does not know whether speed or delay is better. [B]

80   Tá fáth le gach nidh.
There is reason for everything. [B]

18

81 Ná fág an sionnach ag buachailleacht na ngéach.
Don't leave the fox herding the geese. [M]

81 Ná fág an sionnach ag buachailleacht na ngéach.
Don't leave the fox herding the geese. [M]

82 Bíodh teinidh agat fhéin
Nó teana do ghoradh leis an ghréin.
Have a fire of your own
Or else depend on the sun for a warming. [M]

83 Is fheárr treabhadh mall nó gan treabhadh idir.
To plough late is better than not to plough at all. [M]

84 Tá dhá lá san earrach comh maith le deich lá san
fhóghmhar.
Two days in spring are as good as ten days in the harvest.
[M]

85 Na bain tuibhe de do thigh féin le sglátaidh a chur air
thigh fir eile.
Do not take the thatch off your own house to put slates on
another man's house. [MA]

86 Féuch nach n-dean tu droch-amharc air.
Take care lest you cast the evil eye on him. [MA]

87 Ná bris do loirgín air sdól nach bh-fuil ann
do shlighe.
Do not be breaking your shin on a stool that is not in
your way. [MA]

88 Ná tóg me go d-tuitidh me.
Do not lift me till I fall. [MA]

89 Is feárrde de'n chailleach a goradh, acht is misde
di a losgadh.
The hag is the better of being warmed, but the worse of
being burned. [MA]

90   Ní cóir gearran éasgaidh a ghréasughadh.
     It is not right to urge an active horse. [MA]

91   Is maith a t-each a shásuigheas gach marcach.
     It is a good horse that pleases every rider. [MA]

92   Tá sneag an cheapaire nar uaith tu ort.
     *You have got the hiccup from bread and butter you
     never ate.* [MA]

93   Ná cuir ghob a g-cuideachta gan íarraidh.
     Never thrust your beak into company without invitation.
     [MA]

94   Cha d-tainig fear an eadarsgáin saor a ríamh.
     The intermeddler never came off safe. [MA]

95   Biann eagla na teine air a leanabh dóithte.
     A burnt child fears the fire. [MA]

96   Chan sgéul rúin a chluinneas triúir.
     A story that three people hear is no secret. [MA]

97   Ma's maith leat síochaint, cairdeas, a's moladh,
     Eisc, faic, is fan balbh.
     If you wish for peace, friendship and praise,
     Listen, look and be dumb. [MA]

98   An té nach ngabhaidh comhairle, glacaidh se
     comhrac.
     He who will not take advice will take a quarrel. [MA]

99   Ná taisbean do fhiacal 's an áit nach d'tig leat greim
     a bhaint a mach.
     Do not show your teeth where you cannot give a bite.
     [MA]

100 Is fearr fuigheall ná bheith air easbuidh.
     Better have the leavings than have nothing at all. [MA]

96   Chan sgéul rúin a chluinneas triúir.

A story that three people hear is no secret. [MA]

101 Is fearr 'na aonar ná bheith a n–droch–chuideachd.
     It is better to be alone than in bad company. [MA]

102 Cha n–é lá na gaoithe lá na sgolba.
     The windy day is not the day for fastening the thatch.
     [MA]

103 Ná dean cró a roimhe na h–arcaibh.
     Do not build the sty before the litter comes. [MA]

104 Ma's milis a mhil, ná ligh–sa de'n dréasoig i.
     Though honey is sweet do not lick it off a briar. [MA]

105 Ná beannuigh an t–íasg go d–tiocaidh se a d–tír.
     Do not bless the fish till it gets to the land. [MA]

106 Mur rinne tu do leabaidh, luidh uirrthi.
     As you have made your bed, lie on it. [MA]

107 Is fearr pilleadh as lár an atha ná bathadh 'sa tuile.
     *It is better to turn back from the middle of the ford than to
     be drowned in the flood.* [MA]

108 An té nach g–cuireann 'sa n–earrach, cha bhainneann
     se san fhoghmhar.
     *He that does not sow in the spring-time will not reap in the
     harvest-time.* [MA]

109 Amharc romhad sul a d–tabhraidh tu do leum.
     Look before you leap. [MA]

110 Is mairg a leigeas a rún le cloidh.
     Woe to the man that entrusts his secret to a ditch. [MA]

111 An té nach g–cuiridh snaim, caillidh se
     a cheud ghreim.
     He that does not tie a knot will lose his first stitch. [MA]

112 Is cóir nidh a thaisgidh le h-aghaidh na coise galair.
It is right to lay something by for a sore foot. [MA]

113 Salachaidh aon chaora chlamhach sréud.
A single scabby sheep will infect a flock. [MA]

114 An té fhanas a bhfad a muigh, fuarann a chuid air.
The man that stays out long, his dinner cools. [MA]

115 Chan fhuair an madadh ruadh teachdaire a riamh a
b'fhearr ná é féin.
The fox never found a better messenger than himself. [MA]

116 Is breállan an té nach nglacfadh airgead a d'fhu-
ralochádh air.
He is a fool that will not take money that is offered to him.
[MA]

117 Is fusa sgapadh ná cruinniughadh.
It is easier to scatter than to gather. [MA]

118 Ná cuntais na sicinidh no go m-beidh siad leigthe.
Do not count the chickens until they are hatched. [MA]

119 Faghann na h-eich bás, fhad a's bhios a féur a' fás.
The horses die while the grass is growing. [MA]

120 Tarruing do lamh comh reidh a's thig leat as béul
a mhadaidh.
*Draw your hand out of the dog's mouth as easily as you
can.* [MA]

121 Déin connradh do reir sparáin.
Let your bargain suit your purse. [OL]

122 Ní hinniúchtar fiacla an eich do bronntar.
The teeth of a horse given as a present are not scrutinised.
[OL]

123 Mairg do-ní deimhin dá bharamhail.
Woe to him who deems his opinion a certainty. [OL]

124 Ní thig luas is léireacht le chéile.
Speed and precision do not agree. [OL]

125 Cuimhnig sul a labharfair, agus féach rót sul a léimir.
Think before you speak, and look before you leap. [OL]

126 Fearr teithe maith ná droichsheasamh.
A good retreat is better than a poor defence. [OL]

127 Ná nocht t'fhiacla go bhféadfair an greim do bhreith.
Do not show your teeth until you can bite. [OL]

128 Mol gort agus ná mol geamhar.
Praise the ripe field, not the green corn. [OL]

129 Bé théid as nó ná téid, ní théid fear na headaragála.
No matter who comes off well, the peace-maker is sure to come off ill. [OL]

130 Ná gearradh do theanga do sgórnach.
Let not your tongue cut your throat. [OL]

131 Nuair bhíonn do lámh i mbéal an mhadra,
tarraing go réig í.
When your hand is in the dog's mouth withdraw it gently. [OL]

132 Cuinnibh an cnámh is leanfaidh an madra thu.
Keep hold of the bone and the dog will follow you. [OL]

133 Fearr féachain rót ná dhá fhéachain id dhiag.
One look before is better than two behind. [OL]

134 An té ghrádhas an dainseur, cailltear ann é.
He that loveth danger shall perish in it. [OL]

135 Bíodh eagla ort is ní baoghal duit.
Be afraid and you'll be safe. [OL]

Drink and Drunkenness

136 An té ólas acht uisge ní bheidh sé air mheisge.
He who drinks only water will not be drunk. [B]

137 Dearbhráthair leadráracht' ólachán.
Drinking is the brother of robbery. [B]

138 Gnídh tart tart.
Thirst produces thirst. [B]

139 Is milis fion, is searbh a íoc.
Wine is sweet — sour its payment. [B]

140 Sgéitheann fion firinne.
Wine reveals the truth. [B]

141 Chan cuireadh gan deoch é.
It is not an invitation without a drink. [M]

142 Bí ar meisge nó in do chéill congbuigh do
intinn agat fhéin.
Let you be drunk or sober keep your mind to yourself. [M]

143 An úair a bhios an deóch a stigh, biann a chiall
a muigh.
When drink is in, sense is out. [MA]

144 Is giorra deóch na sgeul.
A drink is shorter than a story. [MA]

145 Is searbh d'a íoc an fion ma's milis d'a ól.
Wine is sweet in the drinking but bitter in the paying.
[MA]

146 Beag sochar na sír-mheisge.
     Little profit comes from constant drunkenness. [OL]

147 Bean ar meisge, bean i n-aisge.
     A drunken woman is lost to shame. [OL]

Evil

148 Mairg do gnidh eiteach a's goid.
     It is evil to refuse and steal. [B]

149 Olc ann aghaidh maitheasa.
     Good against evil. [B]

150 Is fear eólus an uilc ná an t-olc gan eólus.
     Better is knowledge of evil than evil without knowledge.
     [MA]

151 Fada iarsma na droichbheirte.
     The effects of an evil act are long felt. [OL]

152 Ní lugha an fhroig ná máthair an uilc.
     Evil may spring from the tiniest thing. [OL]

153 Dein maith i n-aghaidh an uilc.
     Do good in return for evil. [OR]

Fame and Shame

154 Buaine clú 'na saoghal.
     Fame is more enduring than life. [B]

155 Ná mol a's ná cain thu féin.
     Neither praise nor dispraise thyself. [B]

156 Ní náire an bhochtannacht.
     Poverty is no shame. [B]

157 Loiteann aoradh mór-clú.
Satire injures great fame. [B]

158 An té a chailleas a náire gheibh sé a dhánacht.
He who loses his shame gets his boldness. [M]

159 Bhí sé camhail is saoitheamhail gur chaill sé a chliú.
He was gentle and civil until he lost his reputation. [M]

160 Is ball buan do'n donas an náire.
Shame is a constant accompaniment of poverty. [MA]

161 Ainm gan tábhacht.
The name without the substance. [MA]

162 Molaidh an gníomh é féin.
The deed will praise itself. [MA]

163 Is úaisle onoir ná ór.
Honour is more noble than gold. [MA]

164 Lán duirn de shógh, agus lán baile de náire.
The full of a fist of gain, and the full of a village of shame.
[MA]

165 Ma's mór do chliú, cha mhaith.
Though your fame is great it is not good. [MA]

166 Is búaine cliú ná saoghal.
Reputation is more lasting than life. [MA]

167 Is fearr diol tnu ná diol truaighe.
It is better (to be) an object of envy than an object of pity.
[MA]

168 Glacaidh gach dath dubh, acht ni ghlacaidh
an dubh dath.
Every colour will take black, but black will take no colour.
[MA]

169 Da fhaide a's bheidheas tu a muigh, ná beir droch-
     sgéul a bhaile ort féin.
     As long as you are from home, never bring back a bad story
     about yourself. [MA]

170 Is buaine bladh ná saoghal.
     Fame endures longer than life. [OL]

171 Beó duine d'éis a anma, agus ní beó d'éis a einigh.
     A man may live after losing his life but not after losing his
     honour. [OR]

172 Is uaislí in clú ina'n t-ór.
     A good name is more precious than gold. [OR]

Faults

173 Ní fheiceann an duine a locht fhéin.
     A person does not see his own fault. [M]

174 Tá siad fíor mhaith atá gan locht.
     They are truly good who are faultless. [M]

175 Aithnigh cú géur a lócht.
     A sharp hound knows his fault. [MA]

176 Is iomad gron a chithear air a duine bhocht.
     Many a defect is seen in the poor man. [MA]

177 Is maith an séideadh sróine do dhuine, smug fhaiceal
     air dhuine eile.
     It is a good nose-blowing to a man to see snot on the nose
     of another. [MA]

Fighting and Contention

178 Claoidheann neart ceart.

Might subdues right. [B]

179 Feárr deire fleidhe 'na tús bruidhne.

The last of a feast is better than the first of a fight. [B]

180 Is treise gliocas 'ná neart.

Cunning is superior to strength. [B]

181 'Sé fear na fiadhnuise is mó chidh an racan.

It is the stander-by who sees most of the quarrel. [MA]

182 Is cruaidh an cath ó nach d-tig fear innsidh an sgéil.

It is a hard fought battle from which no man returns to tell the tale. [MA]

183 Cha dearna se poll nar chuir mi-se táirne ann.

He did not make a hole that I did not drive a nail into. [MA]

184 Iomad na lamh a bhaineas a cath.

It is the multitude of hands that gain the battle. [MA]

185 An té a bhualadh mo mhadadh, bhualadh se mé féin.

He that would beat my dog would beat myself. [MA]

186 Troid chaoracha maola.

A fight between hornless sheep. [MA]

187 Ná seachain a's ná h-agair an cath.

Do not either shun or provoke a fight. [MA]

188 Biann marbhadh duine eadar dhá fhocal.

The killing of a man may be between two words. [MA]

30

186 Troid chaoracha maola.
A fight between hornless sheep. [MA]

189 Théid focal le gaoith, a's théid buille le cnáimh.
A word goes to the wind, but a blow goes to the bone.
[MA]

190 Is uiris dearga ar aithinne fhórloisgthe.
Burning embers are easily kindled. [OL]

191 Ní gnáth cosnamh iar ndíth tighearna.
Rarely is a fight continued when the chief has fallen. [OL]

192 D'fhear cogaidh comhalltar síocháin.
To a man equipped for war peace is assured. [OL]

193 Gach sluagh nach saigh, saighfidher.
Every army that attacks not will be attacked. [OR]

194 Ní sluagh neach ina aonar.
A solitary man makes not an army. [OR]

195 Luighidh iolar ar uathadh.
Many overpower few. [OR]

196 Ní fríth, ní fuighbhither, breithemh bus fíriu cathráe.
There has not been found, nor will there be found, a juster judge than the field of battle. [OR]

197 Ussa éc earnbás.
Any death is easier than death by the sword. [OR]

Folly

198 Déirc d'a chuid fhéin do'n amadás.
An alms from his own share is given to a fool. [B]

199 Aithnigheann óinmhid locht amadáin.
A foolish woman knows the faults of a man fool. [B]

200 Aimideacht geárr is sí is feárr.
The less of folly the better. [B]

201 Bidh ádh air amadán.
     Even a fool has luck. [B]

202 Ceann mór na céile bige.
     Big head, little sense. [B]

203 Diomhaoireas miar amadáin.
     Idleness a fool's desire. [B]

204 Treid bodaigh le sluagh.
     A clown's fight against a host. [B]

205 Briseadh gach uile dhuine fuinneag dó féin, mur
     dubhairt an t-amadan.
     Let every man break a window for himself, as the fool said.
     [MA]

206 Tabhair a rogh do'n m-bodach, agus 's é a díogadh a
     thoghfaidh se.
     Give a clown his choice and he will choose the worst. [MA]

207 Tabhair-se sin damhsa, is bí féin it óinsig.
     Give that to me, and be a fool yourself. [OL]

Food

208 Beathadh an staraidhe fírinne.
     Truth is the historian's food. [B]

209 Feárr a oileamhair 'na a oideachas.
     His feeding (has been) better than his education. [B]

210 Ní thig leat d'arán a bheith agad agus a ithe.
     You cannot have your bread and eat it. [B]

211 Searbh an t-arán a ithear.
     Eaten bread is sour. [B]

212 Ta se amhuil a's mala pioba, cha seineann se go
m–beidh a bholg lán.
*He is like a bag-pipe, he never makes a noise till
his belly's full.* [MA]

213 An té d'uaith an fheóil, óladh sc an brot.
He that has eaten the flesh-meat may drink the broth.
[MA]

214 Is maith an sgeul a líonas bolg.
It is a good story that fills the belly. [MA]

215 Cha líontar an bolg le caint.
The belly is not filled by talking. [MA]

216 'N uair a bhios bolg a chait lán, ghnidh se crónan.
When the cat's belly is full, she purrs. [MA]

217 An rud do thógfadh duine, 'sé mharódh duine eile.
One man's meat is another man's poison. [OL]

218 An úair is gainne an meas 's é is fearr a bhlas.
When the fruit is scarcest, its taste is sweetest. [MA]

Fortune and Misfortune

219 Is caol a thigeas an t-ádh acht 'nna thuilte
móra thigeas an mio-ádh.
*In slender currents comes good luck, but in rolling torrents
comes misfortune.* [B]

220 Ní lia an sonas 'ná an donas ann orlaibh thríd.
Fortune comes not without misfortunes inch for inch. [B]

221 Tá lán mara eile ins an fhairge.
There is another tide in the sea. [M]

222 As a choire anns a teinidh.
     Out of the pot into the fire. [MA]

223 Baitear a long ann a n-aon pheacaidhe.
     A ship is sunk on account of one sinner. [MA]

224 Is bliadhain shóghmhuil shocharaidh
     Bliadhan róghmhuil sceachairidh.
     *An abundant year of haws is a prosperous and profitable
     one.* [MA]

225 Ceatha Iobráin a neartuigheas na saorclann.
     April showers strengthen the buttercups. [MA]

226 Is fearr an t-ágh maith ná éirigh go moch.
     Good luck is better than early rising. [MA]

227 Is fearr a bheith sona ná críonna.
     It is better to be lucky than wise. [MA]

228 Ma's fada a bhios an t-ágh, thig se fa dheireadh.
     Though luck may be long in coming, it comes at last. [MA]

229 Ann's a deireadh thig a biseach.
     The luck comes in the end. [MA]

230 Léig an donas chun deiridh, a n-dúil s' nach
     d-tiocaidh se choidche.
     *Leave the bad luck to the last, in hopes that it may never
     come.* [MA]

231 Biann a mhi-ágh féin a' brath air gach duine.
     Every man has his own little bad luck awaiting him. [MA]

232 An té a bhios síos buailtear clóch air, a's an té a bhios
     súas óltar deóch air.
     *The man that is down has a stone thrown at him, and the
     man that is up has his health drunk.* [MA]

225 Ceatha Iobráin a neartuigheas na saorclann.

April showers strengthen the buttercups. [MA]

233 An nidh nach n-ithtear a's nach ngoidtear, gheabhar é.
The thing that is not eaten, and not stolen, will be found.
[MA]

234 Char dúnadh dorus a ríamh nar fosgladh dorus eile.
There was never a door shut but there was another opened.
[MA]

235 Ta iasg 's a bh-fairge ni's fearr ná gabhadh a ríamh.
There is fish in the sea better than ever was caught yet.
[MA]

236 Is fearr muinighin mhaith ná droch-aigneadh.
Good hope is better than bad intention. [MA]

237 Is minic a bhi dubhach mór air bheagan fearthana.
'Tis often there has been great darkness with little rain.
[MA]

238 Is fearr suidhe gearr ná seasamh fada.
A short sitting is better than a long standing. [MA]

239 Iomarcaidh d'aon nidh, 's ionann sin 's gan aon nidh.
Too much of one thing is the same as nothing. [MA]

240 Is fearr marcaigheachd air ghabhar ná coisigheacht
ó fheabhas.
Riding on a goat is better than the best walking. [MA]

241 Is fearr teine bheag a ghoras ná teine mhór a losgas.
A little fire that warms is better than a big fire that burns.
[MA]

242 Ma's gasta an gearr-fhiadh, beirthear fa dheireadh air.
Though the hare is swift she is caught at last. [MA]

243 Is maith a saoghal é ma mhaireann se a bh-fad.
It is a very good time if it lasts. [MA]

244 Fanann duine sona le séun, agus bheir duine dona
dubh-léum.
*The lucky man waits for prosperity, but the unlucky man
gives a blind leap.* [MA]

245 Minic do caileadh long lámh le cuan.
Often has a ship been lost close to the harbour. [OL]

246 An té chuireas, 'sé bhaineas.
He that sows will reap. [MA]

247 Ní gheabhar an cú go n-imthigh an fiadh.
The hound is not found until the deer is gone. [MA]

248 Sabhálann greim a n-ám dhá ghreim.
A stitch in time saves two stitches. [MA]

249 Ní i gcomhnuidhe mharbhann daidín fia.
It is not every day that daddy kills a deer. [OL]

250 Fearr an mhaith atá ná an dá mhaith do bhí.
*Better one good thing that is than two good things
that were.* [OL]

251 Fearr amhail ná dóith.
Better 'it is' than 'it may be so'. [OL]

252 Ag duine féin is fearr fhios cá luigheann a bhróg air.
The wearer knows best where the shoe pinches him. [OL]

253 Ar uairibh thigid na hanacraí — is fearr san ná a
dteacht an éinfheacht.
*It is well that misfortunes come but from time to time and
not all together.* [OL]

254 Mairg do báitear am an anfa; tigeann an ghrian
i ndiaidh na fearthana.
*Pity the man who is drowned during the tempest, for after
rain comes sunshine.* [OL]

255 Tar éis dubhaidh tig soineann.
     After gloom comes fair weather. [OL]

256 Teas gréine is gar do dhubhadh.
     Sunshine follows gloom. [OL]

257 An bláth chuireas an choill di, tig a
     ionshamhail uirthi.
     The wood will renew the foliage it sheds. [OL]

258 Níl tuile ná trághann.
     Every tide has its ebb. [OL]

259 Dá fhaid lá, tigeann oidhche.
     The longest day has an end. [OL]

260 Ní fhaghann sagart balbh beatha.
     A dumb priest does not get a livelihood. [OL]

261 Fearr leath-bhairghean ná bheith gan arán.
     Half a loaf is better than no bread. [OL]

262 Trí chomhartha an duine dhona, .i. urradhas,
     eadaragáil agus finné.
     *The three signs of an unfortunate man, — going bail, inter-
     vening in disputes, bearing testimony.* [OL]

263 Ní bhí an tubaist acht mar a mbí an spréidh.
     Misfortune comes only where wealth is. [OR]

Friendship

264 Aithníghthear caraid a g-cruadhtan.
     Friends are known in distress. [B]

265 Dearbh carad roimh riachtannas.
     Prove a friend ere necessity. [B]

261 Fearr leath-bhairghean ná bheith gan arán.

Half a loaf is better than no bread. [OL]

266 Gan lón, gan caraid.
     Without store, without friend. [B]

267 Gnidheann ciste cathrannacht.
     Wealth creates friendship. [B]

268 Gnidheann bladar caradas.
     Flattery begets friendship. [B]

269 Ní car gach bladaire.
     Every flatterer is not a friend. [B]

270 Ní buan cogadh na g-carad.
     The fighting of friends is not lasting. [B]

271 Ní easbha go dích cáirde.
     No want compared with the loss of friends. [B]

272 Cha robh caora chlamhach air a t-sréud a ríamh, nar
     mhaith leithi comráda bheith aici.
     *There was never a scabby sheep in a flock that did not like
     to have a comrade.* [MA]

273 Ni h-eólus gan iontuigheas.
     *There is no knowing a person without living in the same
     house with him.* [MA]

274 Na tréig do charaid air do chuid.
     Do not desert your friend for your meat. [MA]

275 An té a luidheas leis na madraidh, éireochaidh se
     leis na dearnadaidh.
     He that lies down with the dogs will rise up with the fleas.
     [MA]

276 Is maith an sgathan súil charad.
     The eye of a friend is a good looking-glass. [MA]

277 A n-am na ciorra aithnighear an charaid.
In time of need the friend is known. [MA]

278 Seachain is ná taobhuig, is ná tabhair an
t-aitheantas ar aonrud.
Be on your guard against taking sides, and on no account
sacrifice your friends. [OL]

279 Togh do chuideachta sul a suidhfir.
Choose your company before you sit down. [OL]

280 Ní coidreamh go híntigheas.
To know a person one must live in the same house
with him. [OL]

281 Seachain droch-chuideachta.
Shun evil company. [OL]

282 Innis dam do chuideachta is neósad cé hé thu.
Tell me your company and I'll tell who you are. [OL]

283 Maith í an charaid, acht gé holc bheith 'na heasba.
Friendship is good, though absence from friends is painful.
[OL]

284 Tástáil do dhuine muinteartha sul a dteastóidh sé uait.
Prove your friend before you have need of him. [OL]

285 Deireadh cumainn comhaireamh.
Reckoning up is friendship's end. [OR]

Gambling

286 Fearr mac le himirt féin ná mac le hól.
Better even a son given to gambling than a son given
to drink. [OL]

287   Súil le cúiteamh do lomann an cearbhach.
      The expectation of recouping himself is what beggars
      the gambler. [OL]

288   Súil le cúitiughadh a mhilleas a cearbhach.
      It is the hope of recompense that ruins the card-player.
      [MA]

Generosity

289   Is bog reidh gach duine fa chraicion dhuine cile.
      Every man is very obliging with other men's hides. [MA]

290   Cha robh bolg mór fial a ríamh.
      A big belly was never generous. [MA]

291   Roinn mur do dhaoine, a's ná fag thu féin falamh.
      Share as your family do, so as not to leave yourself empty.
      [MA]

292   Cuir an ceart 'roimh an bh-féile.
      Put justice before generosity. [MA]

293   Fiú oineach mall druideam 'na chuinnibh.
      Generosity which is dilatory is worth going to meet. [OL]

294   Adeir siad ná deaghaidh fial go hiofrann.
      A generous man, they say, has never gone to hell. [OL]

God

295   Is giorra cabhair Dé 'ná'n torus.
      God's aid is nearer than the door. [B]

296   Is goirid a bhéadh Dia ag léigheasughadh gach loit.
      God could quickly cure all injuries. [M]

297 Chan ionann bodach is Dia.
God is not the same as a big wealthy man. [M]

298 Is buidheach le Dia an umhluigheacht.
Humility is grateful to God. [M]

299 Ní do gach duine a bhearas Dia inntleacht.
It is not to everyone God gives cleverness. [M]

300 Cha bhiann Dia le mi-rún daoine.
God takes no part in the bad designs of men. [MA]

301 Char dhruid Dia bearn a riamh nach bh-fosgoladh
se bearn eile.
God never closed one gap that he did not open another.
[MA]

302 Char órduigh Dia béul gan biadh.
God never ordained a mouth to be without food. [MA]

303 Cha n-é gach aon n-duine d'ar órduigh Dia sponóg
airgid ann a bhéul.
*It is not every one that God ordained should have a silver
spoon in his mouth.* [MA]

304 Cuidigheann Dia leis a té a chuidigheas leis féin.
God helps him who helps himself. [MA]

305 Stiúir gach maitheasa grádh Dé.
The love of God directs everything good. [OL]

306 Giorra cabhair Dé ná an doras.
God's help is nearer than the door. [OL]

307 Túis na heagna namham Dé.
The fear of God is the beginning of wisdom. [OL]

308 Roinneann Dia na subháilcí.
God shares out good things. [OL]

309 An té ná múineann Dia ní mhúineann daoine.
     He who is not taught by God, is not taught by man. [OL]

310 Labraid duine, innisid Dia.
     Man talks, but God sheweth the event. [OR]

Gratitude and Ingratitude

311 Da g–cuirinn gruaig mo chinn faoi n–a chosa, cha
     sásochadh se é.
     *If I were even to put the hair of my head under his feet it
     would not satisfy him.* [MA]

312 Is buidh le bocht a bh–faghann.
     The poor are thankful for what they get. [MA]

313 Mairg ná cuimhnigheann ar an arán d'íosadh sé.
     Woe to him who remembers not the bread he eats. [OL]

Health

314 An rud reamhar do'n mhnaoi bhreóite.
     Give the dainty bit to the sickly woman. [MA]

315 'Si a chneadh féin is luaithe mhothuigheas
     gach duine.
     It is his own wound that every man feels the soonest. [MA]

316 Ní fuláir deachmhadh na sláinte dhíol.
     One must pay health its tithes. [OL]

Hindsight and Foresight

317 Foillsightear gach nidh le h–aimsir.
     By time is everything revealed. [B]

318 Ní h-ealadha go léightear stair.
No science till history be read. [B]

319 Is maith an fáidh deireadh an lae.
The end of the day is a good prophet. [M]

320 Is tuar fearthana alt áilleog.
A flock of swallows is a sign of rain. [MA]

321 Is a g-cionn na bliadhna innsidheas iasgaire
a thábhachd.
*It is at the end of the year that the fisherman can tell his
profits.* [MA]

322 Mol a dheireadh.
Praise the end of it. [MA]

323 Is maith a sgéulaidhe an aimsir.
Time is a good historian. [MA]

324 Thainig tu an lá a n-déigh an aonaigh.
You have come the day after the fair. [MA]

325 Fál fa'n ngort a n-déigh na fóghala.
Putting a fence round the field after the robbery. [MA]

326 A n-déigh 'aimhleis do chithear a leas
do'n Eirionnach.
After misfortune the Irishman sees his profit. [MA]

327 Cha d-tuigear feum an tobair no go d-téid se
a d-tráigh.
The value of the well is not known till it dries up. [MA]

328 Tar éis a chítear gach beart.
It is afterwards events are understood. [OL]

Honesty and Dishonesty

329 Saoileann gaduidhe na g-cruach gur sladaidibh
     an sluagh.
     The man that steals stacks thinks all the world thieves.
     [MA]

330 An uair a thuiteas rógairidh a mach, tiocaidh duine
     macanta air a chuid féin.
     When rogues fall out an honest man will get his own. [MA]

331 Is beag a ta eadar an chóir a's an eugcóir.
     There is but little between justice and injustice. [MA]

332 Cha deanann balbhan bréug.
     A dumb man tells no lies. [MA]

333 Is fearr fuighleach madaidh ná fuighleach mogaidhe.
     Better the leavings of a dog than the leavings of a mocker.
     [MA]

334 Ceannuig an droch-dhuine, is ní baoghal duit an
     duine macánta.
     *Buy the trickster and you need have no fear of the honest
     man.* [OL]

335 Adeir siad go gcanann meisge nó fearg fíor.
     Drunkeness and anger, it is said, speak truly. [OL]

Humility and Boldness

336 Féudaidh an cat amharc air an righ.
     A cat may look at the king. [MA]

337 Is maighistreas a luchog air a thigh féin.
     The mouse is mistress in her own home. [MA]

336 Féudaidh an cat amharc air an righ.

A cat may look at the king. [MA]

338 Is teann gach madadh air a charnan féin.
     The dog is bold on his own little heap. [MA]

339 Is teann an madadh gearr a n-áit a m-biann
     a thathaigh.
     The cur is bold in the place where he is well known.
     [MA]

340 Cha deachaidh se air sgath an tuir leis.
     He did not go behind the bush with him. [MA]

341 Is fálta duine a g-clúid dhuine eile.
     A man is shy in another man's corner. [MA]

342 Ghnidh suidhe ísioll goradh árd.
     A low seat makes a high warming. [MA]

343 Is minic a fagadh an té bu mhó mheisneach, a's
     thainig a deireóil saor.
     *Many a time the most confident person has been left in the
     lurch when the humble one has got off safe.* [MA]

344 Beidh nidh ag an sárachan, 'n úair a bhios an
     náireachan falamh.
     *The pertinacious man will get something when the shame-
     faced will go empty.* [MA]

345 Ná biodh do theangaidh fa do chrios.
     Do not keep your tongue under your belt. [MA]

Hunger

346 Gnath ocrach faochmhar.
     The hungry man is usually fierce. [B]

347 Maith an t-anlan an t-ocrus.
     Hunger is a good sauce. [B]

348 Ní chuimhnigheann an chú ghortach air a coileáin.
The hungry hound thinks not of her whelps. [B]

349 Is annamh bí tart agus ocras le chéile.
Seldom are hunger and thirst found together. [M]

350 Bíonn fear ocrach feargach.
A hungry man is peevish. [M]

351 Cha líonann beannacht bolg.
A blessing does not fill a belly. [MA]

352 Ní thuigeann an sáthach an seang.
The satiated man does not understand (the feelings of) the hungry man. [MA]

353 Cha chuimhnigheann a fear cíocrach a chú go m-beidh a bhrú féin lán.
The hungry man does not remember his hound till his own belly is full. [MA]

354 Is maith an t-annlann an t-ocras.
Hunger is a good condiment. [MA]

355 Is fearr leith-bhuilín ná a bheith falamh gan aran.
Half a loaf is better than being entirely without bread. [MA]

356 Foghnaidh go leór comh maith le féusda.
Enough serves as well as a feast. [MA]

357 Ní thuigeann an sáthach an seang, nuair bhíonn a bholg féin teann.
The man whose stomach is well filled has little sympathy with the wants of the hungry. [OL]

Inevitability

358 Cha dual grían gan sgáile.

There is not usually sunshine without shadow. [MA]

359 An té a m-beidh se 'n chineamhuin a chrochadh, ni
bháithtear go bráth é.

He whose fate it is to be hanged will never be drowned.
[MA]

360 An té a'r 'n-dán dó an donas, is dó féin a bhaineas.

*If a man be doomed to have bad luck it is on himself (only)
it falls.* [MA]

361 Fa bhun a chrainn a thuiteas a duilleabhar.

It is at the foot of the tree the leaves fall. [MA]

362 Chan 'uil coill air bith gan a losgadh féin de chríon-
lach innti.

*There is no forest without as much brushwood as will
burn it.* [MA]

363 Trath sguireas an lamh de shileadh, stadaidh an beal
de mholadh.

When the hand ceases to scatter, the mouth ceases to praise.
[MA]

364 An uair a bhios a cupán lán, cuiridh se thairis.

When the cup is full it will run over. [MA]

365 An té fhalaigheas, 'sé a gheabas.

He that hides will find. [MA]

366 Is maith an gearran nach m-baineann tuisle úair
éigin dó.

It is a good horse that does not stumble sometimes. [MA]

367 Chun 'uil tuile ó mheud nach d-traoghann.
However great the flood it will ebb. [MA]

368 Is olc a ghaoith nach séilidh go maith do
dhuine éigin.
It is a bad wind that does not blow well for somebody.
[MA]

369 Is fada an ród nach m-biann casadh ann.
It is a long road that has no turn in it. [MA]

370 Cha bhiann imirce gan chaill.
There is no removal without loss. [MA]

371 Is éigin do leanabh lamhachan sul ma siubhalaidh.
A child must creep before he walks. [MA]

372 Ní sheasuigheann rith d'each maith i gcomhnuidhe.
Even a good horse cannot keep running always. [OL]

373 Nuair is cruaidh don chailligh, caithfe sí rith.
When the old woman is hard pressed she must needs run.
[OL]

374 Dá fhaid bhíonn an crúisgín a' dul go nuig an uisge,
isé chrích a bhrise.
*However long a pitcher goes to the water, it is broken
at last.* [OL]

375 Is caora an t-uan i bhfad.
A lamb when carried far becomes as burdensome as a sheep.
[OL]

Kinship and Heredity

376 An t-uan ag munadh méidleach d'a mháthair.
The lamb teaching its dam to bleat. [B]

377 Gach dalta mar oiltear.
Every nursling as he is nursed. [B]

378 Má's ionmhuin liom an chráin is ionmhuin
liom a h-ál.
If I like the sow I like her litter. [B]

379 Sgíordann éan as gach ealt.
A bird flies away from every brood. [M]

380 Is fada leanas a' duthchas.
Natural disposition runs a long way. [M]

381 Is lom gualainn gan brathar.
A shoulder without a brother is bare. [M]

382 Is mairg a bhíonn's gan dear'thar.
Woe to him who is brotherless. [M]

383 Sá bhaile tá'n gaol.
It is at home the friendliness is. [M]

384 An t-olc gan mhaith a d-tóin a chóimhigh.
The bad and no good on the back of a stranger. [MA]

385 Guid é bheitheá brath air chat acht pisín?
What would you expect from a cat but a kitten? [MA]

386 Is de'n g-cat a t-earbull.
The tail is part of the cat. [MA]

387 An easgainn ag ithe a 'rubaill.
The eel eating her own tail. [MA]

388 Is olc seanadh an éin a thréigeas a h-éunlaith féin.
The bird has little affection that deserts its own brood. [MA]

389 Is tibhe fuil ná uisge.
Blood is thicker than water. [MA]

390 Ma 's dubh, ma 's odhar no donn,
Is d'a meannan féin bheir a habhar a fonn.
Whether it be black, dun or brown,
It is its own kid the goat loves. [MA]

391 An nidh a chi an leanabh, 'sé a ghnidh an leanabh.
The thing the child sees is what the child does. [MA]

392 Char bhris cearc na n-éun a sprogaille a ríamh.
A hen with chickens never yet burst her craw. [MA]

393 Théid gach éun le n' alt fein.
Every bird goes along with its own flock. [MA]

394 Eunlaith an aon eite a n-éinfheacht ag eitiollaigh.
Birds of one feather flying together. [MA]

395 Is tréise an dúchas ná an oileamhuin.
A hereditary disposition is stronger than education. [MA]

396 Gach cat a n-déigh a chineáil.
Every cat after its kind. [MA]

397 Briseann an dúchas tre shúilibh a chait.
The natural disposition of a cat bursts out through her eyes.
[MA]

398 Thug se ó dhúchas é, mur thug a mhuc a rútail.
He got it from nature, as the pig got the rooting in the
ground. [MA]

399 Guid é dheanadh mac a chait acht luchóg a ghabháil?
What would the son of a cat do but catch a mouse?

400 Gach eún mur oiltear é, ars' an chuach a' dul 's a
neanntáig.
Every bird as he has been reared, said the cuckoo, as she
went into the nettle. [MA]

401 Budh dual do laogh an fhiaidh, rith a bheith aige.
     It is natural for the fawn of a deer to have fleetness. [MA]

402 An rud fhásas 's a g-cnáimh, ni féadar a dhíbirt
     as a bh-feóil.
     *The thing that grows in the bone is hard to drive out
     of the flesh.* [MA]

403 Beiridh cearc dhubh ubh bhán.
     A black hen lays a white egg. [MA]

404 Chan úaisle mac righ ná a chuid.
     The son of a king is not nobler than his food. [MA]

405 Saoileann gach éun gur b'é a chlann féin is deise air a
     g-coill.
     *Every bird thinks her own young ones the handsomest in
     the wood.* [MA]

406 Ná bi 'g 'ul eadar a craiceann 's a crann.
     Do not go between the tree and its bark. [MA]

407 Is ionmhuin leis a chat iasg, acht ni h-áill leis a
     chrúba fhliuchadh.
     The cat likes fish, but does not like to wet her paws. [MA]

408 Geal leis an bhfiach ndubh a gheárrcach féin.
     The raven thinks its own chick white. [OL]

409 Cad do dhéanfadh mac an chait acht luch
     do mharbhadh?
     What would a young cat do but kill a mouse? [OL]

410 Cionnus bheadh an t-ubhaillín acht mar bheadh
     an t-abhailín?
     How could the apple be but as the apple-tree? [OL]

411 Gach dalta mar oiltear.
     A foster-child is as he is brought up. [OL]

407 Is ionmhuin leis a chat iasg, acht ni h-áill
   leis a chrúba fhliuchadh.
   The cat likes fish, but does not like to wet her paws. [MA]

412 Treise dúthchas ná oileamhain.
     Hereditary instinct is stronger than up-bringing. [OL]

413 Minic ná deaghaidh bó le bó dhúthchais.
     Often a cow does not take after its breed. [OL]

414 Buan fear 'na dhúthaig.
     A man lives long in his native place. [OL]

415 Mairg do bhíonn i dtír gan duine aige féin.
     *Woe to him who is in a country where there is none to
     take his part.* [OL]

416 Níor cailleadh fear riamh i measg a chuaine.
     A man never fails among his own people. [OL]

417 Is bádhach lucht éinchine.
     People of the same stock are friendly. [OL]

418 Is le fear na bó an laogh.
     The calf belongs to the owner of the cow. [OR]

419 Beodha gach bráthair fri aroile.
     Active is one kinsman against another. [OR]

Law

420 Is feárr carad 's a g-cúirt 'ná bonn sa sparán.
     A friend at court is better than a groat in the pocket. [B]

421 Deireadh gach sean-mhallacht, sean-ghearran bán.
     The end of every old curse is an old white horse. [MA]

422 Ní théid dlighe sa bhuille ná buailtear.
     A blow that is not struck is not actionable at law. [OL]

Laziness

423 Is fuath le Dia an fallsoir.
God hates a lazy man. [M]

424 An té nach n-oibrigheann dó fhéin oibreóchaidh sé
do dhaoinibh eile.
He who will not work for himself will work for others. [M]

425 Is olc an chearc nach sgríobfaidh dí fhéin.
She's a bad hen that will not scrape for herself. [M]

426 Ní tabharfaidh tú scór ba a choidhche do do ingin.
You will never give your daughter a score of cows. [M]

427 Ta uallach mhic léisge ort.
You have the burden of the son of laziness on you. [MA]

428 Is trom an t-uallach an fhallsachd.
Laziness is a heavy burden. [MA]

429 Ghnidh codladh fada tón lom.
Long sleep makes a bare back. [MA]

Life and Living

430 Is feárr a oileamhain 'na a thogbháil.
His living is better than his education. [B]

431 Más maith leat a bheith buan caith fuar agus teith.
If you wish to live old, make use of hot and cold. [B]

432 Más maith leat a bheith buan caith uait agus teith.
If you wish to live long, fling off and flee. [B]

433 Ni'l 'sa t-saoghal so acht ceo.
This life is but a vapour. [B]

434 Ní beatha go dul air neamh.
     No life till going up to heaven. [B]

435 Is milis an rud an t-anam.
     Life is sweet. [OL]

Love

436 Fearg a's fuath namhuid un deagh-ghráidh.
     Anger and hatred are the enemies of true love. [B]

437 Is dall an grádh baoth.
     Self-love is blind. [B]

438 Chan fheil liaigh no léigheas ar a' ghrádh.
     There is no physician or cure for love. [M]

439 Is doiligh fhághail ó gheasaibh a' ghrádha.
     It is hard to escape from the bonds of love. [M]

440 Fuarann gradh go grod.
     Love cools quickly. [MA]

441 Falaigheann gradh gráin, agus chi fúath a lán.
     Love conceals ugliness, and hate sees many faults. [MA]

442 Ceileann searc ainimh is locht.
     Love hides blemishes and faults. [OL]

443 Bíonn an grádh caoch.
     Love is blind. [OL]

444 Ní breitheamh comhthrom an grádh.
     Love is not an impartial judge. [OL]

445 Ní dheaghaidh fear meata chun baintighearnan.
     Faint heart never won fair lady. [OL]

446 I ndiaidh an tsochair do bhíonn an grádh.
     Love pursues profit. [OL]

447 Mo ghrádh thu, a rid agat.

   I love you — what you have! [OL]

448 Iomad don aithne

   méaduigheann sé an tarcuisne.

   Too much familiarity breeds contempt. [OL]

449 Is airdhenu screci sírshilliuth.

   Constant gazing betokens love. [OR]

Manners

450 Cha mhilleann deagh-ghlór fiacal.

   A sweet voice does not injure the teeth. [MA]

451 Chan fhaghann fear mogaidh modh.

   A mocker is never respected. [MA]

452 Cúairt go h-anamh go tigh do charaid, a's fanach
   gearr goirid ann.

   *Pay visits to your friend's house seldom and stay but a
   short time there.* [MA]

453 Thig se gan iarraidh mur thig a dó-aimsir.

   He comes like the bad weather, uninvited. [MA]

454 Ná cuir do chorran a ngort gan iarraidh.

   *Do not bring your reaping-hook to a field without
   being asked.* [MA]

455 Fearr béasa ná breághthacht.

   Better good manners than good looks. [OL]

Marriage

456 Mairg d'ar b' céile baothán borb.

   It is sad for the person whose partner is a haughty varlet. [B]

457 Pós bean oileann is pósfaidh tú an t–oileann uilig.
Marry an island woman and you marry the whole island.
[M]

458 Pós bean as gleann is pósfaidh tú an gleann uilig.
Marry a woman out of the glen and you marry the
whole glen. [M]

459 Losg si a gual a's cha dearna si a goradh.
She burnt her coal and did not warm herself. [MA]

460 Is teóide do'n m–brat a dhúbladh.
A blanket is the warmer for being doubled. [MA]

461 Fál fa'n meur 's gan ribe fa'n tóin.
A ring on the finger and not a stitch of clothes on the back.
[MA]

462 Mairg ná deineann cómhairle deaghmhná.
Woe to him who does not have the counsel of a good wife.
[OL]

Meanness

463 Is gnáth sanntach á riachtanas.
The covetous man is always in want. [B]

464 Is mairg a bhidheann go h–olc 's a bheith go bocht na
dhiaigh.
It is a poor thing to be stingy, and to feel troubled after
the little that is given. [B]

465 Ní fhághann lámh iadhta acht dorn dúnta.
A closed hand gets only a shut fist. [B]

466 Saint bun gach uile.
Avarice is the foundation of every evil. [B]

467 Féile dartacháin.
A niggard's generosity. [B]

468 An té is mó fhosglas a bhéul, sé is lugha
fhosglas a sporán.
*The man that opens his mouth the most, opens his heart
the least.* [MA]

469 Bíann a donas a m-bun na stiocaireacht.
Bad luck attends stinginess. [MA]

470 Béul eidhnáin, a's croidhe cuilinn.
A mouth of ivy and a heart of holly. [MA]

471 Ní bhfaghann dorn dúnta ach lámh iadhta.
A shut fist gets only a closed hand. [OL]

472 Iongnadh fear aitheanta na locht do bheith go holc
uim an mbia.
*'Tis strange that one who is so quick at discovering faults
should himself be so stingy about food.* [OL]

473 Ar eagla na heasba is maith bheith coimeádtach,
acht ní abraim leat bheith leamh ná spadánta.
*It is a good thing to be economical in order to guard against
want; but I do not recommend you to be mean or niggardly.*
[OL]

Necessity

474 Ní bh-fuil dlíghe aig riachtanas.
Necessity has no law. [B]

475 Brosnuigheann airc intleacht.
Necessity urges invention. [MA]

476 Ní théid dlighe ar an riachtanas.
Necessity knows no law. [OL]

477 Riachtanas máthair na géir-intleachta.
     Necessity is the mother of invention. [OL]

478 Is dénta áil d'égin.
     A virtue must be made of necessity. [OR]

Nobility and Royalty

479 Déan suas leis an uaisleacht a's déan cuman léithe,
     acht air do chluas na bhí fuar le do dhuine bocht féin.
     Associate with the nobility, and be in favour with them; but
     on no account be cold with your own poor people. [B]

480 Ní leun go díth tighearna.
     No misery like the want of a lord. [B]

481 Ní uaisleacht gan subhailce.
     No nobility without virtue. [B]

482 Ní file go flaith.
     No poet till a prince. [B]

483 Ní uabhar uaisleacht.
     Nobility is no pride. [B]

484 Rioghacht gan duadh, ní dual go bh-fagthar.
     A kingdom is not usually got without trouble. Without
     pains, without gains. [B]

485 Umhlacht d' uaisleacht.
     Obedience (is due) to nobleness. [B]

486 Uaisleacht gan subhailce.
     (No) nobility without virtue. [B]

487 Righ mifhoghlamtha is asal corónta.
     An illiterate king is a crowned ass. [B]

487 Rígh mífhoghlamtha is asal corónta.

An illiterate king is a crowned ass. [B]

488 Ní faghthar saoi gan locht.
     Not (even) a nobleman is to be found without a fault.
     [MA]

489 Uaisle éisteas le healadhain.
     It is a sign of nobility to listen to art. [OL]

490 Is sleamhuin leac dorus tigh móir.
     The door-step of a great house is slippery. [MA]

491 Is rí cech slán.
     A sound man is a king. [OR]

492 Is treise flaith fiora.
     A prince is mightier than men. [OR]

493 Dlighidh ollamh urraim ríogh.
     A king should honour a man of letters. [OR]

Obligations

494 Maith air shean n-duine, maith air án-nduine, agus
     maith air leanabh, trí neithe a théid a mógha.
     *A good thing done for an old man, for an ill-natured man,
     or for a child, are three good things thrown away.* [MA]

495 Fearr sean-fhiacha ná sean-fhala.
     Better old debts than old grudges. [OL]

496 Mairg chailleas a gheasa.
     Woe to him who fails in his obligations. [OL]

497 Ná bris do gheasa.
     Break not your vows. [OL]

Opportunism

498 As na síor-thathaigh thig na cathaighe.

From frequent opportunities come temptations. [MA]

499 Trath 'ghoireas a chuach air a sgeathach lom, diol do bhó a's ceannaigh arbhar.

When the cuckoo cries on the bare thorn bush, sell your cow and buy corn. [MA]

500 An lonn dubh a sheineas go binn 's na Faoilligh, gulaidh se go cruaidh 's a Mart.

The black-bird that sings sweetly in February will lament bitterly in March. [MA]

501 Chaithfeadh an té gheabhas súas leis eirigh go móch.

The man who will overtake him must rise early. [MA]

502 Sábháil an fóghmhar faid do bheidh an ghrian suas.

Make hay while the sun shines. [OL]

503 Glac an mhuc ar chois nuair gheóbhair.

Catch the pig by the leg when you can. [OL]

504 Tóg an liathróid ar a' gcéad hop.

Take the ball at the hop. [OL]

505 Uain nó taoide ní fhanaid le haonduine.

Time and tide wait for no man. [OL]

506 Ní fhanann tráigh le fear mall.

The ebb-tide waits not for a dilatory man. [OL]

507 Ní fhanann muir le fear ualaigh.

The sea does not wait for a man with a load. [OL]

508 Fuiris fuine i n-aice mhine.

It is easy to knead when meal is at hand. [OL]

502 Sábháil an fóghmhar faid do bheidh an ghrian suas.

Make hay while the sun shines. [OL]

Patience

509 Foighid leigheas seanghalair.
Patience is the cure for an old complaint. [B]

510 Gheobhaidh foighid a furtacht.
Patience will get its comfort. [M]

511 Ná mol a's ná di-mol goirt
No go d-ti go rachaidh an mhi mheodhan thart.
*Neither praise nor dispraise growing crops till the month of
June is over.* [MA]

512 Char uaith na madaidh deireadh na bliadhna go fóill.
The dogs have not eaten up the end of the year yet. [MA]

513 Is subhailce an fhoighid nach d-tugann náire.
Patience is a virtue that causes no shame. [MA]

514 Buadhann an fhoighde ar an gcinneamhain.
Patience conquers destiny. [OL]

515 Is ceirín do gach lot an fhoighde.
Patience is a plaster for every wound. [OL]

516 Is ceirín do gach uile chréacht an fhoighde.
Patience is a plaster for all sores. [OL]

517 Anaidh fear sona le séan.
The lucky man waits for prosperity. [OR]

518 Is fada le fear furnaidhe.
One who is waiting thinks the time long. [OR]

Peace

519 Níor chuaidh fear an eidirsgán as.
The peace-maker never lost. [B]

520 Níor cheannuig éinne riamh an tsíocháin ach an té
     ná fuair í.
     *No one has ever bought peace save the man who has not
     got it.* [OL]

521 Is ferr síth sochocad.
     Peace is better than (even) easy warfare. [OR]

Perception

522 Air lí ní breith fear gan súilibh.
     A man without eyes is no judge of colour. [B]

523 Aithnigheann mórbhacht modhamhlacht.
     Greatness knows gentleness. [B]

524 An dubh gné ní h-aithruighthear é.
     The black hue is not changed. [B]

525 Dall air lí ní breitheamh fíor.
     A blind man is not a true judge of colours. [B]

526 Fearr dá shúil 'ná aon t-súil.
     Two eyes are better than one. [B]

527 Olc síon nach maith d'aon.
     Bad blast that is not good to (some) one. [B]

528 Ocht n-amharc ocht g-cuimhne.
     Eight views, eight recollections. [B]

529 Tóirigheacht a ghadhair a's gan fios a dhath.
     Looking for one's hound without knowing its colour. [B]

530 Uisge a d'iomchur a g-criathur.
     To carry water in a sieve. [B]

531 Athruighthear gné na h-aimsire.
     The appearance of the times is changed. [B]

532 Tá sé comh mín le crúbh cait.

He is as gentle as the claws of a cat. [M]

533 Té is deise do theach a' phobaill

Té is maille do'n aifrionn.

He who is nearest the chapel is the latest at Mass. [M]

534 Cha bhfaghthar uisge coistreacha i dteampall Gallda.

Holy water is not found in a Protestant church. [M]

535 Dá mhéad an lán mara tráigheann sé.

However high the tide it ebbs away. [M]

536 Glac an saoghal mar thig sé leat.

Take the world as it comes. [M]

537 Tá misneach an bhru'deargain aige.

He has the courage of the robin. [M]

538 Sin spanóg i mbéal fir eile.

That's a spoon in another man's mouth. [M]

539 An rud nach éigin aoibhinn.

The thing that is not a necessity is pleasant (to do). [M]

540 Má's fuar an teachtaire,

Is fuar an freagra.

If the messenger is cold,

The answer is cold. [M]

541 Is suai'neach béal druidthe.

A shut mouth is peaceful. [M]

542 Is fusa tuitim ná éirigh.

Falling is easier than rising. [MA]

543 Leigeann gach duine uallach air a ngearran éasgaidh.

Every one lays a burden on the willing horse. [MA]

537 Tá misneach an bhru'deargain aige.

He has the courage of the robin. [M]

544 Maireann an chraobh air a bh-fál, a's cha mhaireann
an lamh a chuir i.
*The tree in the hedge remains, but not so the hand that
planted it.* [MA]

545 Is de 'n imirt mhaith a choimhcad.
Watching is part of good play. [MA]

546 'S é an gaduidhe is mó is fearr a gnidh crochadair.
It is the greatest thief that makes the best hangman. [MA]

547 Is olc a breitheamh air dhathaibh dall.
A blind man is a bad judge of colours. [MA]

548 An t-sóid is dó-fhaghala, 'sé is áille.
The jewel that is hardest to be got is the most beautiful.
[MA]

549 An nidh is anamh, is é is iongantaighe.
The thing that is scarce is the most wonderful. [MA]

550 An té 'bhios buaidheartha, biann se bogadaigh,
'S an té 'bhios aedharach, biann se 'mogadh air.
The man who is troubled sits rocking himself,
While the man who is cheerful makes game of him. [MA]

551 Ta dhá chionn a teud a's cead a tharruing aige.
He has got the two ends of the rope and leave to pull.
[MA]

552 Is iomadh gléus ceóil a bhíos ann, ars' an fear a robh a
trumpa maide aige.
*There's many a sort of musical instrument, said the man
who had the wooden trump.* [MA]

553 Ní lia tir ná gnathas.
There are not more countries than there are customs. [MA]

554 Geinn d' í féin a sgoilteas a darach.
It is a wedge made from itself that splits the oak-tree. [MA]

555 Tá fuasgladh gach ceisde innti féin.
The explanation of every riddle is contained in itself. [MA]

556 Ni'l ó mheud a teachdaire nach móide
na gnothuighe.
The greater the messenger the more important the affair.
[MA]

557 Iobrán bog braonach a bheir boinne bá a's age
caoraigh.
A soft dropping April brings milk to cows and sheep. [MA]

558 Chan mur shaoiltear a chriochn'ar.
Things do not end as we expect. [MA]

559 'Sé an t–éadach a ghni an duine
The clothes make the man. [MA]

560 Suairc an taobh a muigh agus duairc an taobh a stigh.
Civil outside and churlish inside. [MA]

561 Is minic grána greannmhar, a's éadan deas
air mhísteáir.
*Often an ugly person is agreeable, and a mischievous one
has a handsome face.* [MA]

562 Ma's olc a dath, is maith a dreach.
Though the complexion is bad, the countenance is good.
[MA]

563 Cha chluinnean se an nidh nach binn leis.
He does not hear what is not pleasing to him. [MA]

564 Is anamh bhios teangaidh mhilis gan gath ann a bun.
A sweet tongue is seldom without a sting at its root. [MA]

565 Biann borb faoi sgéimh.

A violent disposition may be under a beautiful form. [MA]

566 Biann cluanaidhe a n–deagh–chulaidh.

A deceiver may be dressed in fine clothes. [MA]

567 Cionn éireóige air shean–cheirc.

A pullet's head on an old hen. [MA]

568 Is binn gach éun ann a dhoire féin.

Every bird is melodious in his own grove. [MA]

569 Bíann adharca móra air bhá a bh–fad ó bhaile.

Cows far from home have long horns. [MA]

570 Is glas na cnuic a bh–fad uainn.

Distant hills appear green. [MA]

571 Cruthughadh na putóige a h–ithe.

The proof of a pudding is the eating of it. [MA]

572 Is mall gach cos air chasan gan eólus.

On an unknown path every foot is slow. [MA]

573 Moladh gach duine an t–ath mur gheabhaidh se é.

Let every man praise the ford as he finds it. [MA]

574 Mór–thaidhbhseach iad adharca na mbó tar lear.

Far-off cows have long horns. [OL]

575 Is glas iad na cnuic i bhfad uainn.

Distant hills are green. [OL]

576 Ceileann súil an ní ná faiceann.

The eye hides what it does not see. [OL]

577 I n–ithe na potóige bhíonn a tástáil.

The proof of the pudding lies in the eating of it. [OL]

578 Bíonn cluasa ar na clathacha.
     Fences have ears. [OL]

579 Ná leig do rún le cloidhe.
     Tell your secret not even to a fence. [OL]

580 Tuigeann fear léighinn leathfhocal.
     A man of learning understands half a word. [OL]

581 Ní beag nod don eolach.
     A contraction is sufficient for a scholar. [OL]

582 Dealg láibe nó focal amadáin.
     A fool's remark is like a thorn concealed in mud. [OL]

Pollution

583 Ma ghradhann tu an t-aoileach, ni fhaic tu
     dúragan ann.
     If you are fond of dung you see no motes in it. [MA]

584 Is leithide an bualtach satail ann.
     Trampling on dung only spreads it the more. [OL]

Poverty and Riches

585 Bidheann rath air an t-sruimhleacht.
     There is prosperity attending slovenliness. [B]

586 Is coim cabán do bhoicht.
     A hut is a palace to a poor man. [B]

587 Ní náire an bhochtannacht.
     Poverty is no shame. [B]

588 Sáruigheann eagnacht gach saidhbhreas.
     Wisdom excels all riches. [B]

589 Bídh cluid fheascair ag an t-saithraidhe.
The man of plenty has a quiet homestead. [B]

590 Is bocht a' rud fear fiúntach folamh.
It is a sad thing (to see) a decent man poor. [M]

591 An té a bhfuil uisge is móin aige
Tá an saoghal 'na shuidhe ar an tóin aige.
*He who has water and turf (in his own land) has the
world sitting square.* [M]

592 Ní chlaoidhtear fear na h-éadála.
The man of means is not conquered. [M]

593 Ní thuirstear fear na h-éadála.
The man of means is not wearied. [M]

594 An bocht fá'n chladach agus an sardhbhir fá mhintibh.
*The poor man for the gutter and the rich man for the fine
path or roadway.* [M]

595 Milleann a bhoichtineacht a choingeall.
Poverty destroys punctuality. [MA]

596 Chan'uil aige acht o'n láimh go d-ti an beul.
He has nothing but from hand to mouth. [MA]

597 Is iomad sift a dheanas duine bocht sul a sgabadh
se tigh.
*Many a shift the poor man makes before he will give up
his house.* [MA]

598 Is baile bocht, baile gan toit gan teine.
It is a poor village that has neither smoke nor fire. [MA]

599 Millidh an ainnis an t-iasacht.
Poverty spoils borrowing. [MA]

600 Cha seasann sac falamh.
     An empty sack does not stand upright. [MA]

601 Ni baoghal do'n m-bacach an gaduidhe.
     The beggar is in no danger from the robber. [MA]

602 Ní fiú an sógh an té nach bh-fulaingidh
     an-ndóigh tamull.
     *He that will not bear adversity for a while does not
     deserve prosperity.* [MA]

603 Nachar leór do dhuine dhona a
     dhichioll a dheanamh?
     Is it not enough for a poor man to do his best? [MA]

604 Is farsuing béul a bhothain.
     Wide is the door of a little cottage. [MA]

605 Is ait leis na daoine dealbha an bhláthach.
     Needy folks are pleased with buttermilk. [OL]

606 Más le bheith ceirteach dhuit, bí cruinnecheirteach.
     If you must be in rags, let your rags be tidy. [OL]

607 An té ná faghann an fheóil is mór an sógh
     leis an t-anairthe.
     He who does not get meat thinks soup a great luxury.
     [OL]

608 Gach bocht le muir is gach saidhbhir le sliabh.
     Poor men take to the sea, rich to the mountains. [OL]

609 Baodhach le gach bocht a bhfaghann.
     A poor man is pleased with whatever he gets. [OL]

610 Uireasba ní cumha.
     Want makes sadness. [OL]

611 Bochtaineacht níos cumha.
There is no woe to want. [OL]

Procrastination

612 Ná cuir do ghnothuighe ó 'n-diugh
go d-ti a máireach.
Do not put off your business from today till tomorrow. [MA]

613 Is éasgaidhe neóin ná maidin.
Evening is more active than morning. [MA]

614 Deineann gach moch a ghnó.
An early riser gets through his business. [OL]

615 Eusga neóin ná maidean.
Evening is speedier than morning. [OL]

616 Bíonn an fear deireanach díoghbhálach.
A late man brings trouble on himself. [OL]

617 Deineann codla fada tóin leis ag duine.
Long sleep makes a bare breech. [OL]

618 Ná cuir an mhaith ar cáirde.
Postpone not a good action. [OL]

619 Bíonn an aithrighe mhall contabh arthach.
To defer repentance is dangerous. [OL]

Profit

620 Goid ó ghaduidhe, faghail a n-asgaidh.
To steal from a thief is to get for nothing. [MA]

621 Cha n-diolaidh si a cearc a riamh 'sa lá fhliuch.
She never sells her hen on a wet day. [MA]

622 Ní théid cómhar na gcómharsan le chéile.
     Mutual help in farming does not always coincide. [OL]

623 Ní cortar fear na héadála.
     The money-maker is never tired. [OL]

624 Minic chaith duine sprot amach chun breith
     are cholamóir.
     Often has a man cast a sprat to catch a hake. [OL]

Property

625 Sin a chloch a n-áit na h-uibhe.
     That is the stone in place of the egg. [MA]

626 Sin a sóp a n-áit na sguaibe.
     That is the wisp in place of the besom. [MA]

627 Tá do chuid 's do bhuidheachas agad.
     You have both your property and your thanks. [MA]

628 Ná fag fuighleach táilleair do dhéigh.
     Do not leave a tailor's remnant after you. [MA]

629 Is fearr suidhe ann 'aice ná suidhe ann 'áit.
     It is better to sit beside it than in its place. [MA]

630 Bíodh rud agat féin, nó bí in éamuis.
     Have a thing yourself, or else do without it. [OL]

Proverbs

631 Ma thréigear a sean-fhocal, ní bhréugn'ar é.
     *Though the old proverb may be given up, it is not the
     less true.* [MA]

632 Ní sáruighthear na seanfhocail.
     Proverbs cannot be contradicted. [OL]

624 Minic chaith duine sprot amach chun breith
are cholamóir.

Often has a man cast a sprat to catch a hake. [OL]

Reconciliation

633 Ní dheaghaidh rogha ó réiteach.
     Nothing is preferable to reconciliation. [OL]

Sense

634 Cionn mór air bheagan céille.
     Big head and little sense. [MA]

635 Cha robh se air faghail, 'n úair a bhi an chiall
     da roinn.
     He was not forthcoming when sense was distributed. [MA]

636 Is beag a ghaoith nach ngluaisidh guaigín.
     It is a little wind that will not move a giddy-headed person.
     [MA]

637 Is mian le h-amadan imirce.
     A fool is fond of removing. [MA]

638 Tá níos mó ná míola ann a cheann.
     He has more than lice in his head. [MA]

639 Tá fios aige ca mheúd gráinne pónair a ghnidh cúig.
     He knows how many beans make five. [MA]

640 Is trom an t-uallach aineólas.
     Ignorance is a heavy burden. [MA]

641 Is fearr an chiall cheannaighthe ná a faghail
     a n-asgaidh.
     Sense that is bought is better than what is got for nothing.
     [MA]

642 'Si an chiall cheannaighthe is fearr.
     Bought sense is the best. [MA]

643 Ní thigeann ciall roimh aois.

Good sense only comes with age. [OL]

644 Deacair geirrfhiadh chur as a' dtor ná beidh sé.

It is hard to drive a hare out of a bush in which he is not.
[OL]

645 Ní buintear fuil as tornap.

One cannot draw blood from a turnip. [OL]

Silence

646 Air teacht na bh-focal borb is binn beul iadta.

When wrathful words arise a closed mouth is soothing. [B]

647 Is binn é beul nna thosd.

A silent mouth is melodious. [B]

648 Ná bídheadh do ghíomh ó do theangain.

Let not thy act be from thy tongue. [B]

649 Is furas beagan cainte a leasughadh.

It is easy to mend little talk. [MA]

650 Is binn beul 'n thosd.

A silent mouth sounds sweetly. [MA]

651 Deineann ceann ciallmhar béal iadhta.

A wise head makes a closed mouth. [OL]

652 Binn béal 'na chomhnuidhe.

The mouth that speaks not is sweet to hear. [OL]

Speech

653 Leigheas gach brón comhrádh.

Conversation is a cure for every sorrow. [B]

654 Ní fhanann seal mara rabhartha le comhrádh ban.
A spring tide does not wait for women's conversation. [M]

655 Dheanfá sgéal do chlochaibh trágha.
You would make a story out of the stones of the strand. [M]

656 Is maith sgéul go d-tig sgéul eile.
One story is good till another comes. [MA]

657 Tracht air a diabhal, agus taisbeanaidh se é féin.
Talk about the devil, and he will show himself. [MA]

658 Beagán agus a rádh go maith.
Say but little and say it well. [OL]

659 Is gnáthach an rud is giorra don chridhe gurb é is
giorra don bhéal.
What is nearest the heart is, as a rule, nearest the lips. [OL]

660 Níor bhris deaghfhocal béal éinne riamh.
A kind word never broke anyone's mouth. [OL]

661 Gé ná bíonn aon chnámh sa teangain, is minic do
bhris sí ceann duine.
*Though there is no bone in the tongue, it has often
broken a person's head.* [OL]

Trust and Treachery

662 Bidh cluanaidhe a n-deágh-chulaidh.
A deceiver is often in a fine dress. [B]

663 Bidh boirbeacht ann geal gáire.
There is anger in an open laugh. [B]

664 Is treise gliocas 'ná neart.
Cunning is superior to strength. [B]

657 Tracht air a diabhal, agus taisbeanaidh se é féin.

Talk about the devil, and he will show himself. [MA]

665 Ní h-olc aon bheart go m-budh feall.
No action is malicious but treachery. [B]

666 Rúnaidhe cealgach.
A deceitful secret-searcher. [B]

667 Seachain cluanaidhe a's cealgaire.
Shun a prying thief and a deceiver. [B]

668 Sionnach a g-croicean an uain.
The fox in lamb's clothing. [B]

669 Is olc an margadh a bhriseas beirt.
It is a bad bargain that breaks two. [M]

670 Ná tabhair taobh le fear fala.
Trust not a spiteful man. [OL]

671 Mairg 'na mbíonn fear a bhraite 'na chuibhreann.
Woe to him whose betrayer sits at his table. [OL]

672 Cheithre nithe nách tugtha d'Éireannach ionntaoibh
leó, .i. adharc bhó, crúb chapaill, dranna madra agus
gáire Sagsanaigh.
Four things which an Irishman ought not to trust,
— a cow's horn, a horse's hoof, a dog's snarl and an
Englishman's laugh. [OL]

673 Trí nithe nách iontaoibh, — lá breágh insa gheimhre,
saoghal duine chríonna, nó focal duine mhóir gan
sgríbhinn.
Three things that are not to be trusted, — a fine day in
winter, the life of an aged person, and the word of a man of
importance unless it is in writing. [OL]

Truth and Falsehood

674 Beathadh an staraidhe fírinne.
Truth is the historian's food. [B]

675 Imigheann an breug agus fanann an fhirine.
The lie passes away — truth remains. [B]

676 Is searbh an fhírinne, acht is milis an bhreug
air uairibh.
Truth is bitter, but a lie is savoury at times. [B]

677 Ní mhaireann na bréaga acht tamall.
Lies only run a short course. [M]

678 Má's bréag uaim í,
Is bréag chugam í.
If it is a lie as I tell it,
It is a lie as I got it. [M]

679 An nidh a deir gach uile dhuine, caithidh se
bheith fíor.
The thing that everybody says must be true. [MA]

680 Is fearrde a dhearcas bréug fiadhnuise.
A lie looks the better of having a witness. [MA]

681 Meallan a fear bréugach a fear sanntach.
The liar deceives the greedy man. [MA]

682 Ni fiú sgéul gan ughdar éisdeachd.
A story without an author is not worth listening to. [MA]

683 Mhionnochadh se poll thríd chlár.
He would swear a hole through a plank. [MA]

684 Bíann a fhirínne searbh go minic.
Truth is often bitter. [MA]

685 Minic gur sia théid an bhréag ná an fhírinne.
Falsehood often goes farther than truth. [OL]

686 Bíonn an fhírinne féin searbh.
Even truth may be bitter. [OL]

687 Mór í an fhirinne, agus buaidhfe sí.
Truth is great and will prevail. [OL]

688 Ní hionmhuin le Dia an béal bréagach.
God loves not a lying tongue. [OL]

Value

689 An t-seód do-fhághala 's í is áilne.
The rare jewel is the most beautiful. [B]

690 Bidheann blas air ann m-beagán.
The smaller the sweeter. [B]

691 Ceannuigh droch rud a's beidhir gan aon rud.
Buy a bad article and you will be without anything. [B]

692 Is feárr an mhaith atá 'na an mhaith a bhí.
The good that is is better than the good that was. [B]

693 Is feárr greim de chuinín 'na dhá ghreim de chat.
One morsel of a rabbit is better than two of a cat. [B]

694 Fearr mada beo na leon marbh.
A living dog is better than a dead lion. [B]

695 Féadaim ór do cheannach go daor.
I can buy gold at a great price. [B]

696 Is fearr greim de choinin ná dhá ghreim de chat.
One bit of rabbit is worth two bits of a cat. [MA]

697 Olc an chú nách fiú í fead do leigean uirthi.
It is an ill dog that is not worth whistling. [OL]

698 Minic bhí cú mhall subháilceach.
A slow-footed hound often has good qualities. [OL]

699 Is minic bhí braimín gioblach 'na ghillín chumasach.
Often has a tattered colt grown to be a splendid horse. [OL]

Water

700 'Sé an t-uisge is éadomhuine is mo tormán.
It is the shallowest water that makes the greatest noise. [MA]

701 Gach duine a' tarruing uisge air a mhuileann féin.
Every man drawing water to his own mill. [MA]

702 Ard fuaim na n-uisgí éadtroma.
Shallow waters make a great noise. [OL]

703 Rithid uisgí doimhnne ciúin.
Still waters run deep. [OL]

Wealth

704 Feárr clú 'na conách.
Character is better than wealth. [B]

705 Gnidheann ciste cathrannacht.
Wealth creates friendship. [B]

706 Gnidheann saidhbhir réir a aonta.
A rich man acts according to his wish. [B]

707 Gnidh sparan trom croidhe éadtrom.
A heavy purse makes a light heart. [MA]

708 Ní gnáth fear náireach éadálach.

A shamefaced man seldom acquires wealth. [OL]

Wives and Women

709 Go sgaraidh an lacha le linn do snamh;

Go sgarraidh an eala le n-a cluimh báin,

Go sgarraidh an madra le creideamh na g-cnam,

Ni sgarfaidh an gangaid le intin mna.

Till the duck cease on the lake to swim,

Till the swan's down assume a darkish hue,

Till the canine race cease to snatch and fight,

Woman's mind shall not lack guile. [B]

710 Fuar cuman caillíghe.

Cold is an old woman's affection. [B]

711 Gach nidh daor mian gach mnaoi.

Every thing dear is a woman's fancy. [B]

712 Is mairg aig a m-bidheann bean mi-thairbheach borb.

It is a source of regret to have an unthrifty, disdainful wife.
[B]

713 Ní'l nídh níos géire 'na teanga mná.

There is nothing sharper than a woman's tongue. [B]

714 Triur gan riaghal — bean, múile agus muc.

Three without rule — a woman, a mule and a pig. [B]

715 Fiadhnaise a' ghiolla bhréagaigh a bhean.

The lying man's witness is his wife. [M]

716 Fóiridh fear odhar do bhean ríabhach.

A sallow man suits a swarthy woman. [MA]

714 Triur gan riaghal — bean, múile agus muc.

Three without rule — a woman, a mule and a pig. [B]

717 An áit m-biann mna biann caint, a's an áit a
     m-biann géidh biann callán.
     Wherever there are women there is talking; and wherever
     there are geese there is cackling. [MA]

718 Is foisge do bhean leithsgeal ná bráiscin.
     A woman has an excuse readier than an apron. [MA]

719 Chan 'uil ach pleiseám dram a thabhairt do chailligh.
     It is nothing but folly to treat an old woman to a dram.
     [MA]

720 Glacann droch-bhean comhairle gach fir acht a
     fir féin.
     A bad wife takes advice from every man but her own hus-
     band. [MA]

721 Is olc a bhean tigh, inghean na caillighe éasgaidh.
     The daughter of an active old woman makes a bad
     house-keeper. [MA]

722 Ná gabh bean gan locht.
     Never take a wife who has no fault. [MA]

723 Ceannsuigheann gach uile fhear droch-bhean acht a
     fear féin.
     Every man can control a bad wife but her own husband.
     [MA]

724 Deacair taobh thabhairt leis na mná.
     It is difficult to trust women. [OL]

725 Trí éirghe is measa do-ní duine, .i. éirghe ó aifreann
     gan críochnú, éirghe ó bhia gan altú, agus éirghe ó
     n-a mhnaoi féin go nuig á hatharú.
     The three worst flittings — leaving Mass before it is
     finished, leaving table without saying grace and leaving
     one's own wife to go to another woman. [OL]

726 Tá trí saghas ban ann, — bean chomh mí-náireach
leis an muic, bean chomh crostáltha leis a gcirc, agus
bean chomh mín leis an uan.
*There are three kinds of women, — the woman as shame-
less as a pig, the woman as unruly as a hen, and the
woman as gentle as a lamb.* [OL]

727 Na trí ruda is deacra do thuigsint san domhan, —
inntleacht na mban, obair na mbeach, teacht is
imtheacht na taoide.
*The three most incomprehensible things in the world — the
mind of woman, the labour of the bees, the ebb and flow of
the tide.* [OL]

728 Trí shaghas fear go dteipeann ortha bean do thuisgint,
— fir óga, fir aosda, agus fir mheadhon-aosda.
*Three kinds of men who fail to understand woman, —
young men, old men and middle-aged men.* [OL]

729 Na trí nithe is measa i dtig, — báirseach mná, simné
deataig agus an díon a bheith ag leigean tríd.
*The three worst things in a house, — a scolding wife, a
smoky chimney and a leaky roof.* [OL]

730 Trí nithe nách buan, — bó bhán, bean bhreágh,
tigh ar árd.
*Three things that are not lasting — a white cow, a hand-
some woman, a house on a height.* [OL]

731 Trí nithe ná tagann meirg ortha, — teanga mná,
cruite capaill búisteura, airgead lucht carthannachta.
*Three things that never rust — a woman's tongue, the
shoes of a butcher's horse, charitable folk's money.* [OL]

732 Trí nithe chómh maith le nithe níos feárr ná iad, —
claidheamh adhmaid ag fear meathta, bean ghránna
ag dall, droch-éadach ag fear ar meisge.
Three things that serve as well as things that are better — a
wooden sword in the hands of a coward, an ugly wife mar-
ried to a blind man, and poor clothes on a drunken man.
[OL]

Youth and Age

733 Leanbh loisgthe fuathuigheann teine.
A burned child dreads the fire. [B]

734 Is fada cuimhne sean leanbh.
An old child has a long memory. [M]

735 Is furus cleacht a thabhairt do sean-leanbh.
It is easy to teach an old child. [M]

736 Ná codail oidhche sa toigh a bhfuil sean duine pósta
ar mhnaoi óig.
Never sleep a night in a house where an old man is married
to a young woman. [M]

737 Cha robh se go maith, o rinne slat cóta dó.
He was never good since the time that a yard (of cloth)
made a coat for him. [MA]

738 Is búaine an buinneán maoith ná crann bromanta.
The soft twig is more durable than the stubborn tree. [MA]

739 An úair a ghlaodhas a sean choileach, foghlumaidh
an t-óg.
When the old cock crows, the young one learns. [MA]

740 Cha ghabhar sean-éun le cábh.
An old bird is not ca..ght with chaff. [MA]

IRISH SUPERSTITIONS

DÁITHÍ Ó HÓGÁIN

Contents

Foreword — The Mind Engaged

Many folk beliefs are referred to as 'superstitions', with the implication that these are silly ideas in no way connected with common sense or rational thought. However, these beliefs are related to human feeling and to psychological needs, and so — no matter how far-fetched they appear — always have something to tell about our attitudes towards life and towards the world around us.

A survey of folk beliefs makes it clear that they bear witness to two basic human emotions: fancy and fear. They are dramatic by nature, for imagination and insecurity are never-failing sources of drama. They are poetic too, focusing on images to the neglect of conscious analysis, and being carried along by whatever is felt to be cohesive in these images.

It can indeed be claimed that superstitions are nothing more than impressions strongly implanted in the mind due to a kind of speculation which mixes the surreal with the real and confuses the abstract with the concrete. They are preserved, and their hold on the mind strengthened, by assertion in speech and by repetition in practice. Though we need not take them literally, they are always of interest, for man 'hopes and fears all', and the unpredictability of life is just as enduring, as ever-present, as is our fascination with it.

ONE

Man the Summation of All Things

T he sense of self is the most constant one in our experience, and much lore therefore centres on it. The human imagination has long been concerned with aspects of our lives, of our own minds and bodies. Although most of the related superstitions are not validated by modern medical science, they often gave people confidence — illusory, but none the less reassuring — in dealing with matters of immediate personal importance.

THE HEAD IS MASTER TO THE BODY

The head and face, as the most obvious and visible conveyors of personality, were given particular emphasis in body-lore. Many cultures visualised the head as the seat of the intellect but also as the seat of the emotions, because of the expression of human feeling in the face — its paling and reddening, its laughter and tears, its variety of grimaces and contortions.

The fact that the head contains the brain and therefore man's rationalising powers was clear from behaviour and from the results of injury, and perhaps was also known from vivisection. The brain is in Irish called *inchinn*, in the sense of understanding, but a double of it is *meanma*, which has connotations of temperament, and both rationale and feeling are contained in the word *intinn*, for the general mental functioning. Not surprisingly, with this notion of totality, a popular proverb stated that 'The head is master to the body,' meaning that if anything goes wrong with the head, the body will be bound to suffer in some way.

DECISION — THE HEAD STANDS ALONE

In early Irish culture, the head was considered to represent the whole of the person. This attitude is shown in ancient rituals of the Celts, who, even after decapitating a foe in battle, would preserve the head and accord it special respect. Classical writers tell of the continental Celts that they were accustomed to hang the heads of their enemies from the ridge-poles of their tents, and that they brought them along to feasts as if these dead enemies were guests. Early Irish stories tell of heads speaking after death, especially at feasts, where they gave instructions and messages to their listeners.

The head seems to have had particular significance in early Ireland in the context of druids and poets, to whom knowledge of past, present and future was attributed. The famous stone head found at Corleck in Co. Cavan, dating from the Celtic Iron Age, may reflect this: it has three faces, as if to indicate that the seer could simultaneously look into these three dimensions of time.

INFORMATION COMES THROUGH THE EARS, IS DISTILLED IN THE BRAIN, IS REPRODUCED THROUGH THE MOUTH

Early literary sources show that the brain was regarded as the control-centre of the body. This eminently sensible view persisted down through the centuries in folklore. At all stages, of course, there was fanciful elaboration, and various attempts were made to bring the other parts of the head into the scheme of things. For example, the breath was envisaged as a stream which carries the words forward. Since it comes from deep inside the body and returns there, it could be thought of as a kind of liquid of the soul.

To breathe ritually upon an object was to impart something of one's essence to that object. This was an important element in folk healing — for example, it was widely believed in Ireland that thrush of the throat could be cured by a fasting person breathing into the patient's mouth.

THE EAR IS PROPHETIC

Folk tradition held that not just words but other effects could be picked up by one's ear. Thus, if the right ear were warm, it was said that the person was being praised, while heat in the left ear meant that backbiting was taking place. Such notions, described by Pliny as current in ancient Rome, remain popular in modern folklore. A belief common in all parts of Ireland was that if a tiny ringing were heard in the ear, the death of a friend was imminent. An alternative explanation was that a friend in Purgatory in need of a prayer was sending the little bell as a signal.

THE POWER OF THE TONGUE

Words, and the proper crafting of them, have always been considered extremely important in Ireland, where there is deep respect for *dea-chaint* (good speech).

The fancy was that the tongue was the cutter and shaper of words as they passed through the mouth, and people with a long and agile tongue were thought to be very good talkers. Medieval Irish literature claims that poets had two capsules on their tongues — one full of honey for praising, the other full of poison for satirising. By a similar process of thinking, later folklore represents poets as washing their mouths after composing a particularly bitter satire. Children, of course, were often told that a spot on the tongue resulted from telling lies, and were made to wash out their mouths when they used vulgar words.

WORDS CAN EITHER HARM OR HELP

Speech, with its immense social potential, was highly
valued and also greatly feared. There was a very strong
belief in the power of a 'bad tongue' — that is, the tongue
of a malicious and unscrupulous person. 'Envy would eat
away the hills,' went an old saying.

Defamation was also credited with more concrete
effects. It was thought that venomous criticism could actually bring sickness or even death to the victim. False or
sarcastic praise was feared because of its cynical intent and,
accordingly, its sinister nature. Most dreaded of all were
compliments which were 'craving', or laced with envy.
Many stories were told of children being falsely praised
by a covetous neighbour, and as a result falling very ill
or dying.

The tongue could be used in constructive ways also.
Those with a 'silver tongue', for instance, could give great
entertainment and encouragement to their fellows, or
could avail themselves or others in matters of romance by
composing fine songs or rhetorics of love. The positive
side too was expressed in concrete terms, such as in the
belief that a lick of the tongue could heal cuts and burns,
particularly if the tongue had first licked the back of a
lizard — an instance of how exotic actions or materials
were much valued by the popular imagination. The
connection with the lizard probably results from the
widespread notion that this creature is itself tongueless,
and so its wasted tongue 'energy' would be gained by the
person who applied his own tongue to it.

THE SOUL CAN BE OBSERVED

The image of the head as the centre of the life-force, and
of the personality, gave rise to many other ideas. For
instance, stories were told of how the soul could some-

times be seen, in the shape of a little bird, a butterfly or a bee, flying out from the mouth of a sleeping person and returning before he awoke. The person might then describe a dream which he had, a dream based on what the soul saw when it had temporarily left the body. A prevalent belief was that, at death, the soul departed through *log an bhaithis*: that is, 'the hollow in the crown of the head'.

WISDOM, LIKE TRUTH, WILL OUT

The general belief was that wisdom was an innate quality — a sort of shining light of the intellect — with which a small number of people were born and which marked them out from the beginning. Many Irish stories tell of a young genius speaking words of poetry or prophecy soon after his birth, to the astonishment of the adults present.

It was said that there were three qualities which came by nature and could not be properly acquired through learning: *guth, féile agus filíocht* (a singing voice, generosity and poetry).

THE HEAD EXAMINED AND HEALED

All heads, whether of geniuses or of ordinary people, are of course susceptible to illness, which was imagined to be caused by a spirit entering the person and putting his dimensions out of proportion. It was thought that the head should have the same circumference when measured vertically and horizontally, and so in order to cure headaches or nervous tension, it was measured both ways to discover what abnormality had occurred. A bandage or stocking would then be tightened around the head and gently squeezed to bring it back into shape.

A common fancy was that the shape of the head indicated personal characteristics. For instance, a broad brow was taken to mean a very developed intelligence, whereas wrinkles on the forehead meant that a person was prone to worry and anxiety. The head was accorded importance in aesthetic terms too. In both early and modern times, a person with a broad temple, bright forehead and gradually narrowing cheeks was considered very handsome.

The mantic importance of the head was reflected in the widespread belief that cures could be obtained by drinking milk from a skull, and the custom in some areas of swearing oaths on skulls.

BLONDES HELD IN HIGH REGARD

An ancient tendency among the Celtic peoples was to consider fair hair as especially beautiful, deriving from the notion that brightness was a divine trait. Both druids and heroes used lime in order to brighten their hair-colour. The seer-hero Fionn Mac Cumhaill was described as fair-haired — his very name (*fionn*) signifies this; in his case, his hair reflected the shining light of his intellect. Other-world women — who inspired the prophets and poets — were always said to have had hair of that colour.

THE MAGIC OF RED HAIR

Accounts of the early Celts show that red hair was prevalent among them, and this too was held in high regard, even though it could be considered to involve a degree of magical danger. Red, after all, is the colour of fire, one of the most inexplicable sources of support to ancient man, but also one of the most hazardous elements known to him. It is curious that, in later times, red hair was often regarded as an inheritance from the Viking raiders who settled in medieval Ireland.

In a country like Ireland, with varieties of green as the general background, the colour red is rare and therefore stands out clearly to the eye. Similarly, in any given group of people, one with red hair would be noticed. Superstitions tend to centre on the unusual, and particularly the picturesque. Thus, to meet a red-haired woman was often considered a bad portent. The belief was very strong among fishermen, who would turn back home if they met with such a woman when going to sea. Perhaps it was felt that a conspicuous woman might deflect the attention of seafarers from their dangerous tasks!

HAIR INDICATES THE PERSON AND THE DESTINY

Red hair was also taken as an indication of a hot-blooded temperament. Since hair was thought to spring internally from the blood, for it to retain this colour was a reflection of that essential human element in its most productive and heated humour. People tended, and to an extent still tend, to regard hidden traits as being expressed externally in one's physical appearance. Strong and healthy hair, whether on the head or on the body, suggested a high degree of strength and health within the whole person.

Conversely, a decline in one's hair presaged a general decline in well-being. Balding, while it had to be accepted as inevitable, was considered extremely undesirable. An Irish saying has it that 'Baldness is most uncomely, and only blindness is a greater affliction.' A sudden greying or thinning of body hair was wont to cause alarm, as it was taken as a portent of sickness or even death.

STRENGTH AND POWER OF THE PERSON LIES IN THE HAIR

In Ireland, and in several other countries, it was thought highly unlucky for a man to allow a woman to cut his hair or shave his beard, the danger being that he would

thereby lose his strength or even his virility. This belief
may stem from the biblical account of Samson and
Delilah, but the Samson story itself is indebted to ancient
folklore of the Middle East.

Many cultures evince a secret fear of an occult power
residing in women. The ultimate source of this — no
doubt male — notion is difficult to decipher, but some
psychoanalysts would attribute it to the symbolism of the
male 'dying' in sexual intercourse. It is significant also that
many primitive cultures considered women to be especially dangerous when menstruating; the association with
lunar periods increased the feeling that women derived
extra power from their involvement with outside agencies.
Incidentally, it was thought inadvisable in Ireland and elsewhere to cut hair while the moon was waning, as this
would bring about a corresponding decline in the hair.

The ancient Celts wore their hair long in battle, in
the belief that their full power was thereby utilised. Down
through the centuries, military leaders in many countries
have made the trimming of hair and beard obligatory for
their soldiers, principally for hygienic reasons, but perhaps
originally in order to deprive the enemy of the chance of
seizing a soldier's hair in close combat. The Celtic custom
of wearing hair long survived in Ireland for a considerable
time, and men took particular pride in leaving the mous-
tache untrimmed. Various ordinances during the reign of
Elizabeth I sought to compel Irishmen to cut their mous-
taches, but to little avail.

HAIR SHOWS FEELINGS, STATUS AND FATE
Long hair on women was understood to express freedom
and informality, and it was habitually tied up only after
marriage. The hair thus symbolised a woman's sexuality.

A long tradition, indeed, associated hair with sexual attraction — a lock was often given as a love-token, and strands of hair were an important ingredient in love-potions. In a different context, women allowed their hair to hang unkempt when keening the dead. On formal occasions, such as going to church, no woman would allow her hair to straggle; it would be gathered up neatly as a mark of solemnity and respect.

Since of its nature the hair can take on many shapes, its condition was much noted in folk divination. For instance, the 'cow's lick', or tuft of hair standing up over the forehead, was taken as a sign of health and intelligence in a child. On the other hand, a pronounced forelock in a woman, with the hair thinning about it, was called the 'widow's peak', and betokened the death of the woman's spouse in the near future.

HAIR AN INTRINSIC PART OF THE BODY

People were very careful not to throw their severed locks into the fire, for they would feel themselves weaken as the hair burned. It was held that those who allowed their hair to burn would on the Last Day be burning their fingers in an attempt to retrieve it from the fire. This, needless to say, was derived from the Christian doctrine of the resurrection of the body. It was maintained that the best place in which to put discarded hair was a hole in the ground or a hole in the wall, from which it could be collected before the Final Judgment.

This, however, entailed its own difficulty, for if the birds were to discover it and use it in the building of their nests, severe headaches could result for the owner of the hair. Such pain had its own remedy in popular belief, and a cure for both headaches and head-colds was to discover the *ribe tuathail*, a particular strand at the back of the head, and pull it.

THE EYES ARE A WINDOW ON THE MIND

A well-known saying in Irish lists the three most vulnerable parts of the body as 'the eye, the knee and the
elbow'. The eyes have long been considered 'the mirror
of the soul', and folk fancy ranged all the way from the
serious observation that one should be careful with a
person whose eyes expressed a humour at variance with
that of his mouth, to the more flippant one that the eye of
a girl at a dance was as sharp as that of a hawk surveying a
plain or of a hound after a hare! A blue-green eye-colour
was regarded as very attractive, while a grey eye was an
indication of prudence and practicality.

UNUSUAL TYPES OF EYES ATTRACT SUSPICION

Unusual formations of the eyes were mistrusted —
especially where the eyes were very close together or
differed from each other in colour. To nervous and
over-imaginative observers, such facial aspects suggested
some hidden destructive tendency.

Belief in the 'evil eye' was prevalent since antiquity in
many countries. According to this, a glance by some individuals could bring harm to whatever it was cast upon. In
Ireland, it was described as a 'blinking' or a 'cutting' eye.
While the supposed possessor of such an eye was sometimes considered a malicious or covetous person, it was also
thought that one could possess this destructive trait due to
no fault of one's own or without even knowing of it.

Once it became known to an honest person that he
possessed the undesirable trait, he might strive to avoid
doing damage with it. Since it was believed that the object
which first met the eye in the morning would suffer the
full effect of it for that day, he could carefully direct his
first glance at weeds or undergrowth — which would, of
course, wither away as a result of the repeated exposure.

Folk tradition tends to concentrate on the dramatic, and
most stories of the evil eye told of people who used the
attribute maliciously and were therefore to be avoided at
all costs. It was claimed that those who acted treacherously
towards their neighbours did not close their eyes, even
when sleeping. A child, horse or cow which was 'over-
looked' by such a person would pine away and die, and so
it was advisable to procure some defence against the eye,
or some remedy which would neutralise its effect.
Defences and remedies included religious amulets, the
Sign of the Cross, the invocation of God's blessing, and
the more quaint and antique one of spitting.

THE BLESSED POWER OF SALIVA
The use of spittle as a prophylactic was widespread in
human culture, and was very popular in Ireland. Since it,
like the breath, comes from the mouth, it was thought to
contain the essence of one's personality, and therefore of
one's potential. Just as people spat on a wound in order to
clean it and accelerate its healing, they spat on a horse or
cow in the belief that spirits and disease were kept away
by the act.

The spittle of a fasting person was considered particularly efficacious, perhaps because it was felt to contain the
undiluted essence of the person. In a less philosophical
mood, people spat on money in the hope that it would
become more plentiful!

BLOOD IS WHAT WE ARE
The most essential of bodily elements is, of course, the
blood. Because its spilling can cause death, and because it
congeals at death, it was understood in many ancient
cultures to contain the very spirit of life itself. Blood was
considered synonymous with individuality, and so it was

used as a guarantee in agreements and covenants; by signing in his own blood or by mixing it with that of another, the person committed himself totally.

Likewise, based on blood-lines, traits of character were thought to be hereditary or to 'run in families'. A person might be described as having a 'good drop' or a 'bad drop' in him if his actions were seen to be of a type with those of his ancestors.

THE VEIN OF POETRY

The pulse, through which the 'life' of the blood can most clearly be perceived, played an important role in these beliefs in Ireland. It was stressed in the case of poets, whose mystical skills were thought to reside in their own personalities.

The notion was prevalent that there was a special vein of poetry in a poet's body, a *féith na filíochta* which was not found in the bodies of other people. This vein was situated at the back of the head, a fancy which we can take to represent a primitive form of phrenology, but also perhaps to illustrate the 'hidden eye' of a genius. Gaelic poets, according to ancient ritual, composed in darkness, and the back of one's own head is an unseen, or 'dark', part of the body. When the poet began to compose, it was thought that the blood began to pulsate through this vein, and the metre of the poem corresponded to the pulsation.

BREEDING BREAKS OUT

Events in one generation could, through their influence on the blood, have an effect for a long period afterwards. Thus, for instance, if a family were cursed, this could mean harm or misfortune in that family for seven generations. A curious element of this belief was that poetry, as an hereditary gift, would leave a family for seven

generations if it manifested itself in a daughter rather than
a son. This notion presumably owes something to the
change of surname which would occur when the girl
married. Poetry was, in late medieval Ireland, a profession
specific to certain families — such as the O'Dalys, the
Wards, the Keoghs, the Egans and the O'Higgins.

THE IMPORTANCE OF FAMILY

According to folk belief, the Keoghs shared a special
attribute with those who had the surnames Cahill, Walsh,
Darcy or Cassidy. This was that they could, by use of
their blood, heal ringworm, wildfire and other ailments
of the skin.

More generally, it was believed that cures could be
performed by a person whose parents had the same
surname, whatever that name might be. This belief probably derives from a fancy that the juncture of two streams
of the same blood would bring out its inherent life-giving
qualities in extraordinary relief. On a lighter note, children
were told that if a boy and girl, at play, were injured and
their blood intermingled, they were destined to marry
when they grew up.

THE PULSE OF LIFE

The emphasis on blood as the life-force, flowing from the
heart of the individual to the external organs, caused
people to speculate that there was one vein or pulse on
which all others depended. This was known as *cuisle na
beatha* (the pulse of life). It was said that it might manifest
itself in any part of the body, and that if it were struck a
blow when seen to twitch or jump, the person would die.
The old literature refers to this pulse as the *bradán* (salmon)
of life, which warriors might eject from their bodies in the
heat of combat, thereby expiring.

The belief persisted strongly in west Munster, where
the *iasc* (fish) of life was spoken of as travelling around the
body between the flesh and the skin. It was said to
become obvious when one was under some form of strain,
and resembled a nerve-quiver. Stories were told of how,
due to a craving hunger or exhausting work, a particular
person ejected this fish through his mouth, but a quick-
witted companion seized it and prevailed on him to
swallow it again, thus saving his life.

CRYING OUT TO HEAVEN FOR JUSTICE

A belief commonly held abroad as in Ireland was that
blood, since it belonged to the essence of a person, could
bear witness of its loyalty to that person even after death.
It was said, for instance, that the body of a murdered
person would shed blood when the murderer came near
to it, so exposing him. Another prevalent belief was that
grass would not grow on the spot of earth where the
blood of a slain person fell, or conversely that a fine tree
would grow from that spot in honour of the dead.

THE THROBBING HEART

The heart was generally understood as the source of the
emotions, even though these were structured or ration-
alised in the head. Both feelings of affection and feelings
of revulsion and dislike were believed to originate in the
heart, which was said to shake with fear and anger in reac-
tion to hostile circumstances. Emotions were stressed by
saying that they came from *lár an chroí* (the centre of the
heart), or sometimes even from the liver underneath it.
Thus, a common expression of affection in Irish was *a
chara na n-ae istigh* (literally, o friend of the liver inside).

Since the heart was accorded such importance in
human behaviour, blood circulating to the limbs was

believed to carry instructions from it. This idea was reinforced in popular lore by old medical theories concerning
the importance of particular veins, such as the cephalic,
which was in medieval times thought to be the special
conveyor of messages from the heart to the limbs.

THE HAND WHICH HUMANISES

Information could be imparted manually in more ways
than one. The 'life-line', or fold at the base of the thumb,
in both ancient and modern times gave rise to many
fanciful interpretations. If long, it is said to indicate deft-
ness and skill; if deep and unbroken, it portends a long
life; and if crossed by several other lines, it suggests that
one's life will be a varied and eventful one. The hand
being the most industrious part of the body, it was
employed symbolically in communications and in
commerce. Waving, gesticulating and shaking hands are
instances of this, and at markets, an Irish person would
stress his commitment to a bargain by spitting on his
palm before the concluding handshake.

THE 'LITTLE MEN' AT WORK

Each finger had its own name, and there was a tendency
to attribute specific properties to them. To have an index
finger of the same length as the third finger was in several
countries considered a sinister sign, and in Ireland it was
taken to indicate a stern or cruel nature, or alternatively a
propensity for stealing. There was also a belief in many
countries that a special vein runs from the heart to the
third finger on the left hand, and in this way was
explained the custom of wearing a wedding-ring on that
finger. Another fancy was that the long finger on the right
hand had a conduit to the life-centre, and a drop of blood
pricked from it could cure the skin ailment wildfire.

The thumb was particularly valued, for it was thought
to contain a cure for erysipelas and warts. Spittle was put
on it, and it was then applied to the affected part. For a
nose-bleed, a string was tied around the little finger on the
same side as the affected nostril, the idea apparently being
that the blocking of the blood-flow at one extremity of
the hand would cause a similar blocking at the extremity
of the face.

THE FINGERS AS SIGNPOSTS

A general custom, based on Christian imagery, was for the
fingers to be crossed when danger of any type threatened.
To look at a person from behind the extended fingers was
believed to bring him bad luck, perhaps because this
concentrated a hostile glance and made its destructive
power more lethal. Death was thought to be presaged by a
tingling or numbness in the fingers, or by the appearance
of yellow or black marks on the nails. A less startling interpretation was given to white nail-marks, supposedly an
indication that one would soon be undertaking a journey
on the sea.

NAILS, THE ESSENCE EXTERNALISED

The nails were regarded as an intrinsic part of an individual, since they grew from within. Discarded nails, like
discarded hair, could be used by a hostile neighbour to do
magical harm to a person — for instance, by burning
them to cause painful and dangerous illnesses. This seems
to have been the basis for the custom — general
throughout Ireland — of not cutting a baby's nails until he
was twelve months old and therefore past the most
vulnerable phase of his young life.

A play of folk fancy upon the Book of Genesis gave
rise to a curious little idea. This was that the nails, along

with the eyelashes, are the remains of the angelic covering
(called *scéimh aingli*) which Adam and Eve had before their
fall in the Garden of Eden. The presumption was that this
covering would be restored to mankind after the General
Judgment. The larynx in the throat was also widely
believed to be an inheritance from the same Garden,
for Adam — having accepted the apple from Eve —
was said to have hesitated. He did not swallow the
apple, and so it remained in his throat and in the throats
of his descendants!

THE BITING EDGE OF THE BODY
Like the hair and nails, some people feared that teeth
might be missing when the body was resurrected, and so
they kept by them ones which had fallen out or had been
extracted. Others, with more immediate concerns,
worried when a tooth fell out that they would lose the
remainder in a similar manner. So, all over Ireland, it was
advised that such a tooth should be caught in the right
hand and thrown backwards over the left shoulder, which
it was claimed would prevent the precipitate loss of more.
Another superstition was that a dream of losing a tooth
presaged the death of oneself or of a close friend. In this
case, the tooth seems to have been considered symbolical
of the life-force or soul.

VOICE, FACE, CHARACTER AND AMBITION
Other beliefs were derived from simple observation,
coloured by a metaphoric tendency. Thus, a gap between
the two front teeth is still commonly regarded as an indication that a person has a good singing voice, just as a
wide mouth is thought to denote strength in such a voice.
A thin mouth is, rather peremptorily, taken to signify
stinginess and selfishness of character, and pinched cheeks

are often given a similar interpretation. A prominent and pointed chin is humorously dubbed a symptom of forwardness or curiosity.

THE SKIN FEELS AND ANTICIPATES

As the outer layer of the body, the skin was thought to register what was in store from the external world, and various interpretations — some playful — attached to itchings on different parts of the body. Such a sensation on the palms of the hands was often said to indicate that one would before long be the recipient of a letter through the post or, better still, of money; though others interpreted 'itching of the palm' as an uncontrollable desire to spend money. Itching on the knuckles was a sign that one would soon be fighting, on the temples that one would soon have cause to weep, and on the eyebrows that one would soon be drinking whiskey. If a man's nose became itchy, it was said to presage a quarrel with his wife.

STRANGE MARKS, STRANGE REALITY

Finally, marks on the skin were regarded as portents of special significance. A black or brown mark appearing overnight on the arm was thought to result from a pinch by a dead relative, indicating that one would soon be joining that relative in the afterlife. An ordinary mole on the skin was, however, considered a sign of health, and on the face of a young person was thought to enhance good looks.

In former centuries, Irish people, like people of other European countries, considered a red birthmark on the hand or arm of a political or military leader as a presage of remarkable achievements. Particularly dramatic was the notion that a Messianic leader would be born with the outline of a little red cross on his shoulder-blades. The

noble O'Donnell family of Donegal believed for centuries
that a great hero would come of their line and that he
would be known as Aodh Balldearg (Hugh Red-spot).

Perhaps the most dramatic skin-mark in Irish tradition
was that on the forehead of the mythical hero Diarmaid Ó
Duibhne. It was bright and lustrous, and any woman who
saw this *ball seirce* (love-spot) fell hopelessly in love with
the young warrior. As one can well imagine, it became as
much of a hindrance as a help to Diarmaid, and so he
found it necessary to wear his war-helmet low down over
his forehead even when not going into battle! Folklore
claims that when the lady Gráinne, betrothed to
Diarmaid's leader Fionn Mac Cumhaill, saw the *ball seirce*,
she insisted that he elope with her. Fionn never forgave
Diarmaid for this, and through his scheming, caused him
to fight the vicious boar of Benbulben, in which titanic
tussle the handsome young hero was slain.

Two

The World Around Us

Culture, basically, is the way in which people react to their surroundings. It is therefore not surprising that such strong human feelings as curiosity and fear tend to focus on aspects of the environment which are continually, or repeatedly, encountered. When there is a degree of mystery involved, the feeling is increased. As a result, people developed many superstitions concerning the environment; these in time became stabilised as beliefs and are preserved in folk tradition.

GREAT HOUSE OF THE WORLD

The sky, massive and strange, was one of the principal puzzles confronting the mind of man. The mythologies of ancient peoples bear witness to this in many different ways. Here in Ireland, the sky was imagined as a kind of roof covering the earth, as is clear from common expressions in the Irish language such as *frathacha na firmiminte* (the rafters of the firmament), *stua ceatha* (shower-arch, meaning the rainbow) and *cranna na spéire* (the columns of the sky). The sky-roof was, in medieval times, thought to be held up by four huge columns which stood outside the known realms of geography.

To the early Irish saints, earth and sky was one immense construction which reflected the architectural genius of God, 'the beloved smith who built that object, the god of heaven, he is the thatcher who roofed it'. This meant, of course, that there was something outside the sky, the great other-world beyond. One traditional saying describes the stars as 'pin-holes in the heavens, allowing the light out'.

There was therefore a respected basis for speculation that the constellations might have a connection with events which take place on the earth below. The antiquity of the practice of astrology in Ireland is unclear. The Celtic druids were claimed to have detailed knowledge of the moon and stars, and they certainly had developed a sophisticated calendar, but they seem to have made prognostications from the formations of the clouds rather than from the heavenly bodies.

HORSEMAN OF THE HEAVENS

Old Irish literature portrays the sun as a deity who traversed the heavens, a god who drove a fiery chariot, and this status is confirmed by the importance accorded to it in folk belief — where, indeed, it was often referred to as if it were a personage on high. Thus, in Irish the sun is described as going to lie down in the evening, or even going 'into its chair', and the long rays seen before dusk were referred to as 'the legs of the sun'. If affairs were going well with a person, he was said to be 'on the wheels of the sun', and it was a general practice for fishermen to turn their boats sun-wise when setting out to sea. Similarly, hay and corn stacks were constructed 'with the sun' — that is, by working the binding in the same direction as the sun crosses the sky. Even cures were applied with the intention of imitating the sun's course.

HEALTH, WEALTH AND INSPIRATION

The sun, we are told sensibly enough, is 'the clothes of the poor', and it was said that if a person turned his clothes inside out at sunset, he would have luck. If the last of the sun contained precious energy, so, it was thought, must its beginning, and people used to wash their faces in sundew in early morning for health or to improve their complexions. Indeed, according to an old Irish text, sundew is 'a drop impregnated by the sun, and whoever consumes it gains the gift of poetry'.

The fact that the sun is the source of energy on earth could, of course, be guessed at from observation, even in a pre-scientific age. Its importance to the growth of crops and the strengthening of animals is evident. A common saying, 'Happy is the bride whom the sun shines on', meant that she would have a happy married life and be blessed with offspring. It was even believed that a woman would more easily conceive if she lay down for a while in the sunshine.

THE EYE OF DIVINE WITNESS

The ancient pagan Irish adored the sun, a fact recorded by the early Christian writers here. According to these writers, the Irish swore oaths by the heavenly bodies, and such an expression survives in the Irish language — *dar brí na gréine is na gealaí* (by the strength of the sun and of the moon). Early Christianity, aware of the importance attributed by the Romans and others to midwinter, when the sun was 'reborn', decided to celebrate the birth of the Saviour at that time, and thus 25 December was settled upon as Christmas.

THE DANCING FIRE

The appropriation of the sun as an image of Christ, 'the true light of the world', persisted to medieval times, when a superstition spread throughout Europe that on Easter morning the sun danced in the sky with joy at the Resurrection. The sun's image does indeed shimmer on many spring mornings due to the mingling of hot and cold air at the earth's surface. The belief was very strong in Ireland, with people climbing to hilltops to witness the

dancing sun as Easter dawned. It was common also to
watch the reflection of the Easter morning sun in a well or
in a tub of water.

THE SUN LIVES AND DIES

A curious belief was that the sun could quench the household fire if the latter were exposed to it, because sunlight
seems to diminish the light of fire. It was also supposed
that sunlight took the edges off knives and scythes, and
this 'biting' potential is further instanced by references to
butter which melted on a fine summer's day as having
been eaten by the sun.

Given the long-standing recognition of our dependence on the sun, it is not surprising that an eclipse, even
a partial one, caused consternation. People feared that the
hand of destiny had smothered the sun, and for the dura-
tion of the eclipse they prayed that the Almighty might
relent and allow it to shine again. As in many other
cultures, a solar eclipse was taken as a sign of disaster to
come. Such an eclipse in the year 1652 was believed to
have presaged the massive confiscations of Irish land by
the Cromwellian government, and the partial eclipse
of 1846 — following on the near-total one of four
years earlier — was remembered as a portent of the
Great Famine.

THE MOON — MAIDEN AND HAG

The heavenly body which is seen continually to undergo
change was long an object of superstition. The ancient
Celtic druids placed great emphasis on the moon,
arranging their calendar by it, and believing that business
undertaken while it was growing would be successful.

This notion that human affairs depend on the waning
and waxing of the moon persists in many countries. In

Ireland, a child born when there was a new moon was thought to have especially good prospects for health and wealth, and attempts were even made to delay births until that time.

GROWTH AND DECAY FROM ABOVE

The lunar conjunction was generally regarded as an unlucky time, as no moon was then visible and people felt that their good fortune had likewise departed, even if only temporarily. Seeds might, however, be sown in the earth at this time — as they would be concealed for a brief period corresponding to the moon's disappearance, would begin to sprout as the new moon emerged, and would grow copiously with it. Scollops for thatching the roof would be cut as the moon increased, thereby ensuring their continuing strength.

Conversely, any new undertakings would be avoided as much as possible during the waning of the moon — except in cases where loss was actually the desired object. An indirect benefit of the waning moon was that body-sores were believed to decrease in size during it, and warts might disappear altogether. Furthermore, farmers insisted on this time for the castration of their animals, as it was thought to leave the effect of that operation beyond doubt.

The killing of pigs and sheep was carefully arranged according to the same calculations. It was claimed that, if the slaughter took place while the moon was waxing, the bacon or mutton would 'swell in the boil'; if done while the moon was on the wane, it would 'shrink in the boil'. Needless to say, people were much more inclined to spare their money as the moon filled, and to spend it as the moon waned!

THE ETERNAL RETURN

The coming of a new moon was naturally something of a mystery, and attracted much attention. 'On the first night nobody sees it, on the second night the birds see it, on the third night everybody sees it' — so goes an Irish saying. Its coming was not greeted without apprehension, and people were advised to make the Sign of the Cross when they first noticed it. A prayer might also be recited, such as 'God bless the moon and God bless me, I see the moon and the moon sees me.'

There was a strong and enduring country tradition that, with the coming of the new moon, people would kneel and pray in Irish for health, wealth and good fortune. A seventeenth-century German book remarks: 'The wild Irish have this custom, that when the moon is new they squat upon their knees and pray to the moon that it may leave them vigorous and healthy, as it has found them, and they request particularly that they may be safe from wolves.'

MINERALS FROM THE SKY

It was considered lucky to look at the new moon through the clear air, but unlucky to see it through glass. This must derive from the general belief that the body's internal organism is affected by moonlight, a doctrine taught by the alchemists of the Middle Ages. The alchemists further claimed that various minerals were developed in the earth by different planets, the mineral which thus benefited from the moon being silver. A very common superstition was that, when the new moon appeared, a person should turn the money around in his pocket, the idea here seeming to be that a silver coin would flourish if both of its sides were exposed to the moon's rays. Notions about these rays are doubtless behind other beliefs, such as that a person should not look sideways at the moon, but should face it directly.

POTENTIAL AND REPRODUCTION

The most obvious parallel between the moon and human life is the comparable length of its cycle and that of the menstrual cycle in women. As a result, it was thought that women should not stare at the moon, or discuss it in detail, for fear of complications in menstruation. On the other hand, the new moon provided a good occasion to make a wish, and both men and women sought to avail of this in matters of romance. And if one were to tie a little bag of clay around the neck when going to bed, it was said that one's future spouse would appear in a dream.

THE HEAVE AND PULL

It was claimed in folklore that Aristotle failed to gain an understanding of three things: 'the work of the bees, the coming and going of the tide, and the mind of a woman'! Whatever about the other two, ordinary people under- stood that the tides had some connection with the moon, and this provided ready 'proof' of the ubiquitous lunar influences.

Contemplating the strange connection between sea and moon, folklore developed some dramatic ideas. One such was that all water reacts in the same way as the sea; that rivers, for instance, swelled with the full moon, or that water placed in a dish will rise and overflow as the full moon is seen to rise. At the same time, the blood becomes invigorated and a person feels his strength increase. The sap rising in the horns of a cow with the rising moon was believed to cause the horns to soften, allowing the owner to straighten them. Some people even held that stones

softened with the rising moon, and that drops of
perspiration could be seen on them!

SHADOWS IN THE MOONLIGHT

The energy caused by the full moon in all its strength
could, it was thought, be overpowering to the human
spirit, and the belief was widespread in Ireland and abroad
that a person might become over-elated by it and lose his
wits entirely for a while. Such a person was said to have
gone *le gealaigh* (with the moon). In English, indeed, the
word 'lunatic' and its synonym 'moonstruck' derive from
this very ancient belief. Even birds were affected, it being
said that they lived in dread of their shadows at
this time.

Folklore attempted to lessen the apprehension
concerning the full moon by claiming, logically enough,
that the moon was 'full' in a complete sense for only a
very short time, and that its effects would gradually wear
off afterwards. It was often held that a full moon on
Saturday betokened bad weather or some other local
misfortune. However, those with a livelier and more
bizarre imagination claimed that if ever a Saturday full
moon were to coincide exactly with the highest point
of the tide, then the sea would rise and drown the
whole world!

MAN AT THE MERCY OF THE UNKNOWN

Lore of the planets and stars was less alarming, though it
too had its danger-points. For instance, the appearance of
a 'tailed star', or comet, was often taken to presage some
disaster. Due to the influence of medieval astrology, it was
thought that each child was born under a particular planet.
If that planet seemed relaxed and quiet at the birth, he
would have a good life, while if it sparkled, the opposite

would apply. Many stories were told of scholars and
learned people trying to get women to delay giving birth
until the opportune time!

One of the phenomena most noticed in the heavens
was a meteor, or 'falling star', the general belief being that
it represented the release of a soul from Purgatory into
Heaven. It was customary to make the Sign of the Cross
and utter a little prayer of thanks to God when such a
'star' was noticed. In a more secular vein, it was sometimes said that a wish made upon seeing a falling star
would be granted.

A natural explanation was often given, to the effect
that such a 'star' would hit the earth, and that frog-spawn
or similar slimy substances seen on the ground in the
morning were the remains of it.

TWINKLE, TWINKLE, LITTLE STAR

These heavenly bodies were given a romantic significance,
as one might expect. It was often said that if a young man
or woman were to count nine stars each night for nine
consecutive nights, he or she would meet the future
spouse without delay. All of this fanciful lore did not
preclude more rational use of the constellations, for
purposes such as navigating both on land and at sea.
Most important of all in this context was, of course, the
north star, called appropriately in Irish *an réalt eolais*
(the star of knowledge).

Clocks were not in general use in olden times, and
systems were therefore devised to read the time from the
heavens. For instance, the Pleiades (called in Irish *an
Tréidín*, or the little herd) were closely observed, for the
time of night could be read from their position as they
traversed the sky.

WHO IS THERE?

Traditional lore is a mosaic of realistic and fanciful interpretations, and many of the fanciful elements are quite
humorous. Especially notable are the personifications of
natural phenomena. In many countries, the markings on
the moon are interpreted as being the body of a man who
was transported there from the earth. Some Irish versions
of this belief claim that he was a thief who stole a bush
from his neighbours and was sent there as a punishment,
while others state that his offence was to go to collect fire-
wood on Sunday when he should have been in church.

GALE FORCE GATHERING

Perhaps it was the man in the moon who suggested to
people that there might also be a man in the wind. He was
known as *fear na gaoithe* (the wind-man), and was said to
go about in the late autumn knocking the stacks of corn
and hay which lazy farmers had not yet gathered into the
barn. Alternatively, he was said to control and direct
storms, blowing them with a bellows.

A popular Munster story told of how a widow's son,
angry at damage done to his mother's house, once set out
to get satisfaction from the wind-man. He followed the
direction from which the wind was blowing, until he
reached its ultimate source — a large hole in the ground,
where he met the wind-man and made his complaint. The
wind-man had not been aware of the damage he had done
to the widow, and as compensation presented the youngster with a bellows which could control storms. Through
the use of his acquired gift, the youngster grew up to be a
very rich man.

Behind this humorous tale lie ancient attempts to
explain what caused the wind to blow. Many early
mythologies represented storms as resulting from the anger

of the gods or from their furious travelling through the air.
Such an idea was current in Ireland also, the wind being
explained as the moving about of the *sí*, the other-world
beings known in English as the fairies.

Especially feared was a whirlwind, supposed to be the
shock-troops of the fairies moving about. It was said that
one should never look in its direction but should utter a
prayer. The usual term for the phenomenon was *sitheadh
gaoithe* (literally, thrust of wind), but this was pronounced
almost identically with *sí gaoithe* (fairies of wind), which
facilitated the supernatural identification. The whirlwind
was sometimes also alluded to as *deamhain aeir* (literally,
demons of the air), and reference to such frightful beings
was circumvented by substituting as their name *leamhain
aeir* (moths of the air). In the older literature, the swishing
of weapons in battle was claimed to be the screeches of
war-demons.

THE WANDERER THROUGH THE WORLD

A personage was also associated with the phenomenon
known as ignus fatuus, the *tine ghealáin* or 'bright fire' seen
over swampy land at night. This is said to be the soul of a
master-gambler, who defeated the devil at cards but was
refused entry into Heaven because of his profession. He
therefore wanders interminably around the earth seeking a
place to spend eternity and carrying a lantern which gives
off the strange light. He is known in some localities as
'Jack of the Lantern', and in others as 'Will of the Wisp'.

THE SKY A WITNESS TO PAIN

Early Irish literature contains accounts of several person-
ages who seem to have originated in sun-myths, such
as the ancestor deity Eochaidh Aonsúile (One-eyed
Horseman), and the infamous Balar of the Evil Eye, whose

glance destroyed multitudes. There is little evidence for personification of the other heavenly bodies, but folklore commemorates the mythical cow who gave a near-inexhaustible supply of milk. She was known as the Glas Ghoibhneann (that is, the 'grey' of the smith-god Goibhniu). A malicious woman once bet her owner that there was one vessel which the great cow could not fill, and then put a sieve under her. The reliable Glas died trying to fill the sieve, but her effort was so massive, and so copiously did the milk flow from her, that it spurted up to the heavens and coloured an immense cluster of stars. This is the Milky Way!

MYSTERIES OF THE DEEP

The sea too was personified, with a mysterious old man said to control the waters of the deep. When God created the world, he told this man to be careful not to allow anybody to drown, but the man disobeyed these instructions and regularly demands the lives of people as tribute: hence the fatalistic saying, *Bíonn a cuid féin ag an bhfarraige* (The sea must have its due). It was considered unlucky to save a drowning person, for the sea would in time take the rescuer as compensation for its loss of tribute.

According to a story told in Ireland and abroad to explain why sea-water was salty, a ship's captain once got possession of a little magical mill which ground salt. The captain was transporting the mill in his ship, but he was an impatient fellow and could not wait to reach land before testing it. He therefore set it to work, but forgot the word which would make it cease. The weight of salt which the mill produced caused the ship to sink, and ever since it churns out salt from the bottom of the deep.

THE MIGHTY POUNDING HEART

Movement of the sea, what could be perceived as its living
vigour, is expressed by each wave (in Irish, *tonn*). Fairies of
the sea were said to travel in certain waves, which could
thus be made to subside by throwing a knife or some
other weapon at them. One common story told of a man
who in this way injured the eye of a fairy lady, and was
afterwards brought to 'the world under the sea' in order to
remove the offending weapon. The ninth wave out from
the shore is represented, in the old literature and in later
folklore, as a particularly dangerous one. It was known as
the *tonn bháite*, or 'drowning wave'.

No doubt on account of other-world beings residing
in the waves, the ancient Irish poets were believed to be
able to interpret what their voices were saying. There was
a very old tradition that the sea around Ireland had four
great waves, which cried out to foretell a catastrophe, such
as the death of a king. Two of these waves were off the
south-west coast — Tonn Chlíona (in Tralee Bay) and
Tonn Tóime (in Kenmare Bay). The other two were off
the north-east coast — Tonn Tuaidhe (in Rathlin Sound)
and Tonn Ruaidhrighe (in Dundrum Bay).

VOICES FROM THE BEYOND

Speculation concerning unusual or notable sounds was
very common. Thunder was explained as the angels in
Heaven performing drill, while lightning was the flashing
of their swords. A fanciful little explanation for echoes
was that they were the voices of souls in distress. It was
thought that, for some souls, Purgatory could be spent
within the natural landscape, such as in a thorny bush,
under the leaf of a tree, or between the froth and
the river.

Perhaps older is the interpretation of echoes as the speech of fairies, and in hills and rocky places questions were put to fairies in the expectation of some decipherable reply. A more rational, if unscientific, explanation was that an echo was caused by the sound striking against underground water.

DEEDS IN WATER WRIT

Water has long been associated with the other-world. Almost all the rivers of Ireland have female names, and the old literature depicts other-world women as presiding over them. The original mythical idea seems to have been that both land and river represented the body of the tutelary goddess. Little of this survives in folklore, except that spirits and fairies were often encountered on the banks of rivers and lakes.

Water, as an element essential to life, was a favourite abode of the old Celtic gods, and there was a feeling that all types of water were in communion with each other. This is graphically portrayed in a medieval belief that an inland well at Kesh in Co. Sligo had a correspondence with the sea, draining and filling according as the tide ebbed and flowed far away.

THE CLEANSING POWER

The veneration of holy wells, general throughout Ireland down to recent times, is a good example of how the ancient tradition of gods residing in water was adopted into Christian practice. People congregated at these wells, each of which was dedicated to a particular saint, on the feast-day of that saint. Many of the wells were thought to contain cures for specific ailments, a common belief being that, if a cure were to be effected, a little white fish would be seen in the water.

It was frequently said that a holy well had moved
from one position to another — across a road, for instance
— because somebody had fouled it, a piece of lore which
developed to explain the fact that underground water can
vary its point of emergence to the surface.

THE BRINK OF DISASTER

The fear of drowning loomed large in the case of rivers
and lakes as well as in the case of the sea. It was said that
someone was drowned once every seven years in particular rivers or lakes, and it was even told of some rivers
that a voice would be heard periodically crying out and
claiming its sinister due: *Anois an t-am, cá bhfuil an duine?*
(Now is the time, where is the person?)

More pleasant was the belief that fine horses and cattle
could come from a lake, or even from the sea, and mix
with ordinary stock. This lore was especially strong as
regards horses, and many accounts were given of how a
farmer would notice a strange stallion in his fields by a
lakeside. The stallion might turn out to be a great work-
horse or even racer, and the farmer could breed some
splendid stock from it. Usually, however, it was said that
the farmer on some occasion lost his temper with the
animal and struck it, after which it returned to the lake.
Some grisly details might be added, such as that the farmer
swam into the lake to recover it but was savaged by the
horse, and pieces of his body were afterwards seen floating
on the water.

In order to explain how strange beings might come
from the water, extensive use was made of the idea that
some ancient city had been inundated and had sunk to the
bottom of the sea or of a lake. Thus, folklore claimed that
fishermen often heard the sound of music or of bells
coming from under the water; and luminous reflections
on the surface were claimed to be street-lamps far below.

FAR OVER THE SEA

A much older idea — stretching back to the pre-Christian religion of the Celts — was that the other-world was situated on a lonely island in the sea. It was anciently called *Magh Meall* (the Plain of Delight), and also *Tír na hÓige* (the Land of Youth) or *Tír na nÓg* (meaning the land whose inhabitants remain ever-young). Under Christian influence, it became known as *Tír Tairngire* (the Land of Promise). Following the same pattern, folklore claims that there is an other-world island off the west coast called *Uí Bhreasail*, and sun-rays reflected far away on the sea are pointed out to children as this island. More prevalent was the belief that *Uí Bhreasail* was under the water and surfaced only at specific times.

Various names were given in coastal areas to this other-world island. In Co. Clare, it was called *Cill Stoithín* — probably a corruption of Cill Scoithín, meaning the church of Scoithín, who is mentioned in early Irish literature as a celebrated seafaring saint. This island is surrounded by a magical mist, which lifts once every seven years, at which time it can be reached by boat. It is said that the island can be disenchanted by unlocking the door of a fine building which lies there, but the key is hidden in a lake on top of a mainland mountain.

INTRUDERS ON SOLITUDE

Water-horses and water-cattle were usually interpreted as belonging to those fairies who inhabited the aquatic realms. Fairies on land had their own livestock — or if not, were intent on gaining some. As a result, people were anxious when sending their cattle to lonely pastures, for fear they might be 'elf-shot': that is, that the fairies would hit the animals with darts which would cause them to pine away and die and thus be acquired by the farmers of fairyland. Little chips of stone found on the ground — some, in fact, remains of ancient arrowheads — were suspected of being such 'fairy-darts'.

Special care was taken when sending cattle to graze near bogs or on hills, where the fairies were very numerous — for example, the cattle might be struck with a hazel-rod or a branch of the rowan-tree for protection, or blessed with the Sign of the Cross. Fairy-lore is often very close to lore of the dead, and the idea that fairies resided underneath bogs or within mounds and hilltop cairns may be a survival from ancient burial customs.

It should be remarked that, while the association of eeriness or sacredness with lonely locations was intermit- . tent rather than general in Irish culture, it does seem to be a relic of antiquity. For instance, although cases of butter were buried in bogs for purposes of preservation down to recent centuries, this manner of butter-burying seems originally to have represented an offering to placate the spirits of the bogs. A related practice which survived until lately was to throw the first measure into the air at milking-time as an offering to the fairies.

MYSTERIES UNDERGROUND

Indentations in the landscape have long attracted attention and suspicion. The great prehistoric caverns — at Dunmore in Co. Kilkenny, Aillwee in Co. Clare and Mitchelstown in Co. Cork — were anciently known as 'the three dark places of Ireland'. That at Dunmore was, indeed, said to have been inhabited by a monstrous cat, and a drove of such creatures was reputed to have resided in a cave at Rathcroghan in Co. Roscommon. The most famous of all sinister caverns was on an island in Lough Derg in Co. Donegal, called 'St Patrick's Purgatory', which was in the Middle Ages claimed to be the mouth of Hell itself!

More benign was the folk belief that underground passages linked many of the raths and tumuli of Ireland. This belief, which is still very strong, was based on the use in olden times of souterrains, or dug-out caves, for storing food. People have speculated that these were the openings of interconnected tunnels constructed by the *Tuatha Dé Danann*, a magical race which lived underground. Many folk traditions claim that these tunnels were later used by the Irish for purposes of escape from the Elizabethan and Cromwellian armies.

SURVEYING ALL

The custom of climbing hills and mountains at certain festivals is of great antiquity and has not yet died out. The old literature contains several suggestions that communication with the other-world took place at lofty locations — the most celebrated instance being the Hill of Tara in Co. Meath, which from time immemorial was regarded as a sacred site. That hill's name, *Teamhair*, meant 'Spectacle', witness to the fine view it afforded mortals and gods over a broad stretch of the midlands. In an aesthetic sense, Irish tradition claims that poets could find inspiration on hilltops. Due to the force of gravity, proclamations made from such locations were thought to have particular impact.

THE LANDSCAPE PROTESTS

The combined mystical and menacing nature of lonely places caused them often to be regarded with a degree of awe. The most striking instance of this attitude in folklore concerns the *féar gortach* (hungry grass), described as an unlucky patch which may grow in isolated parts of mountainsides. If a traveller were to step on this grass, he would grow weaker and weaker from hunger, and would die unless some remedy were in store. People therefore took

the precaution of bringing a piece of bread with them
when going on long journeys, as this was thought to
counter the magical effect of the hungry grass. This is a
simple example of the spiritualising of a very important
practice in normal life — that of bringing food for a
journey — but there may also be in its background an
element of food-offering to the spirits of the wild.

Another unforeseen hazard of the countryside was
called the *fóidín mearbhaill* or 'wayward sod', which, if
trodden upon, would set a person astray. Most accounts of
this have the mishap occurring at night, with the result
that the traveller would cover long distances and continually end up at the same spot, until the light of day brought
deliverance. Here again is a dramatic expression of a real
dilemma, as losing the way in unfamiliar surroundings
often leaves one travelling in circles.

MAN ASTRAY IN THE WORLD

Another exaggeration of reality was the fairy mist, known
in Irish as *ceo draíochta*, which also puts a person astray until
he finds his bearings. This mist can descend suddenly and
without warning, usually at night and in remote places,
and it was sometimes said to be a portent of one's
impending death. In the old literature, the descent of
such a mist was a preliminary to an adventure in fairyland,
underlining the idea that unfamiliar surroundings can
be the juncture between the ordinary world and the
other-world.

TREE OF THE WORLD

Of trees, the rowan, called in Irish *caorthann* and in
Hiberno-English 'mountain ash', was considered the luckiest species and the most effective against fairy interference. A branch of the rowan was often kept in the cow-

byre, so as to ensure a good milk-yield, and might also be kept in the dwelling-house in the belief that it prevented fire. The *sceach gheal* or whitethorn, on the other hand, was the tree most associated with the fairies, and would never be brought into a building.

The general reluctance to cut down trees, except for some very good purpose, stems from the veneration of them in ancient Ireland. The old literature, indeed, speaks of many a great old tree (called *bile*), which acted as a kind of protector of the landscape. This idea seems to be based on the sheltering function of a tree, and perhaps also on the notion that the sky was held up on columns. Most notable of all was the *Bile Tartain* (at Ardbraccan in Co. Meath), which was an ash of gigantic size said to have existed since the beginning of the world.

THREE

Ourselves and the Others

R ealising that the human race shared the world with
many kinds of creatures, and sensing that different forms
of life were interdependent, people were curious about
the identity and purpose of these other creatures, and there are
a lot of old traditions concerning the various species of fauna.
Very prevalent was the idea that they could congregate for
their mutual benefit, just as humans did. Many countries
have folktales telling of parliaments convened by the animals
and birds. The quadrupeds chose the lion as their king, and
the birds would have elected the eagle but for the fact that the
wren hid in its tail and thereby flew higher, gaining the crown
for itself.

Such a fanciful way of thinking gave rise to many superstitions, most notably that some species were originally human
but had been enchanted long ago into their present forms.
This, to the self-centred human mind, made the secrets of
nature more comprehensible, but folk imagination did not
stop there. The many puzzling features of the world, and
the many unexplained occurrences, led to the idea that the
earth was inhabited also by mystical beings, such as spirits
and fairies, which were as real as the more obvious
physical beings.

THE EXTENDED NOSTRILS

Since they were in closest proximity to people, superstitions abounded concerning domestic animals, their
natures and habits. It was generally believed that horses
had the power to see spirits, and that they would stop
on the road at haunted places and could not be
persuaded to move on. This fancy seems to be based

on observation of the natural skittishness of horses and
of their very keen sense of smell, both of which cause
them to balk at anything they find threatening.
Folklore claimed that if a rider or carter looked ahead
directly between the horse's ears on such an occasion,
he would be able to see the spirit which was there.

DANGER TO PROPERTY

Horses were of great importance in the business and social
life of long ago, and people were very anxious lest any
mishap befall them. So there was a wide range of beliefs as
to how a malicious person might do harm to a neighbour's horse by envious praise or by use of the evil eye.
Possible interference by the fairies, too, was feared, and so
it was usual for an owner to spit on his horse both
morning and night, for the fairies were quite fastidious and
would have nothing to do with anything which had been
soiled. It was also said that the horse sneezed in order to
protect itself from the fairies.

One type of horse was well able to defend itself, if
folklore is to be credited. This was the *fíorláir* (true mare),
defined as being the seventh filly born to its dam without
any colt intervening. Such mares were considered unusu-
ally good workers and gallopers, and neither magic nor
spirits had any effect on them. Indeed, stories were told of
how they could protect their owners from malice and
misfortune. It was said that where the true mare was
dropped by its dam at birth, the four-leaved shamrock
grew. This was known as the *Seamair Mhuire* (the Virgin
Mary's Clover) and was much in demand as a talisman.

THE BLESSED HORSE

Horses were often said to be lucky animals, and people got
them to trample a little on newly sown fields, as this

would cause the seeds to sprout well. The horse's halter
was believed to bring good luck, and was always kept by
the seller when the animal was sold. The value or good
fortune of the animal, which had been enclosed by the
halter, would be retained within that trapping.

THE COW IS LEATHER, MEAT AND MILK

Cattle were, of course, also of great value, and this fact too
was projected onto the other-world. Their owners feared
that the fairies would try to take the cattle, and objects
considered repugnant to the fairies were attached to them.
A favourite method was to tie a rowan-twig to the tail of
a cow, or to rub dung on her udder. Another common
trick was to have the cow inhale smoke, which, it was
believed, other-world beings could not tolerate. However,
cracks in a cow's skin were thought to be caused by fairy
darts, and to be a preliminary to her health fading away.

Cows without horns were said to be good milkers, as
it was believed that horns sapped up the energy of an
animal. Since music was thought to increase cows' yield,
people often sang or whistled while milking. A curious
tradition attached to the keeping of bulls. It was said that
the animal should never be placed in a field where an
echo could be heard, because, on hearing his lowing
repeated, he would think that another bull was present,
would be constantly restive and would pine away.

GOATS AND DONKEYS

Goats are noticeably quick to seek shelter when they sense
the approach of rain, which gave rise to the belief that
they could see the wind. Probably also because of this, as
well as the fact that it can eat many noxious weeds, the
goat was thought of as a sort of guardian-animal, and was
believed to bring luck to a farm. A billy-goat (*pocán*) was

often put among the cattle herd, in the belief that its presence prevented cows from aborting and increased their milk yield. The donkey was also considered a lucky animal, and one deserving of special kindness, because of the widespread belief that it got the cross on its back when it carried Christ long ago.

PECKING ABOUT FOR CLUES

Because of the importance of the egg supply, much lore centred on hens. There is an old saying, 'A whistling woman or a crowing hen bodes no good for God or men!' The crowing, like the whistling, was supposed to be a male trait, meaning that the hen might not produce many eggs, and would be unlucky in a farmyard.

Bad luck was also believed to attach to a white cock, probably because it was the opposite to an all-black one, which was thought to provide protection against danger from all unexpected sources. The black cock crowed to banish spirits, and if hatched in March had especially strong protective power. A common folk legend told of how a seaman once purchased such a 'March cock' from a farmhouse near the shore. As soon as he had taken the bird away, a thunderbolt struck the house.

HIDDEN HOSTILITY

It was claimed that hens had been brought here by the Vikings, and that they had hostile feelings towards the Irish people. This was what caused them continually to scrape on the kitchen floor, in an attempt to set the house on fire. They made preparations each night to return to Scandinavia, but in the morning forgot all their plans! Other animals said to have been brought as pets to Ireland by the Vikings included foxes, which were their dogs, and stoats, which were their cats.

FRIENDS AND FOES

It is said that the dog and the cat argued long ago over
which of them would have first claim on the shelter of the
house. They decided to wager the matter on a race
towards the building. The dog was winning but stopped
to attack a beggar and lost, so the cat ever since has choice
position next to the family fire.

There were, indeed, many superstitions concerning
these household animals. The dog is man's best friend but,
because of its fierce nature, should not be fully trusted.
Therefore, it was said that one should never ask a question
of a dog, lest it answer back. Cats were much valued for
their services against rats and mice, but were believed to
have a secret nature of their own, far removed from that
of people. This springs from observation of the nocturnal
life of cats, and of their ability to see in the dark. It was
said that even the household cat dreams three times each
night of killing its owners, and is deterred from doing so
only by fear of the household dog.

CREATURES OF THE NIGHT

A story was told in Ireland and in other European countries of a man who, returning from the market, was
attacked by a cat. He slew the animal, but before it
expired, it spoke and told him to let the other cats know
what had happened. When he reached home and was
telling his wife of this, the household cat jumped up and
attempted to tear at his throat. It transpired that the dead
animal had been the king of the cats.

Other tales told of how the cats held nocturnal assem-
blies, where they discussed their affairs, and where humans
who eavesdropped might be savagely attacked. It was
believed that cats were very vengeful, and that even quiet
domestic cats consorted with their wild cousins. Wild cats,

formerly common in lonely parts of the country, were said to be vicious fighters and easily to get the upper hand of dogs. A wild cat, it was said, had a claw in its tail, which it used to deadly effect in fights.

TALLY-HO

Of the wild animals, pride of place in storytelling went to the fox, which was celebrated for its cleverness in preying on farmyard fowl and in evading capture. Due to its red colour, which suggested blood-spilling, it was thought to be an unlucky animal to behold when one was beginning some enterprise. Fishermen dreaded to mention the word 'fox' when at sea, probably also because it was felt that so conspicuous a land-animal was inappropriate to that context.

A superstition attaching to some wealthy families — such as the Prestons and the Frenches — was that foxes congregated about their houses, barking mournfully, when a member of these families was about to die.

THE SLEEPLESS KING

The otter was the subject of much fancy. Because of its peculiar eye-folds, it was thought to sleep with its eyes open. One special type, known as the 'king-otter', was said never to sleep. This king-otter had a rare coloration, much of its body being white, but with a cross on its back and its paws and ears black. It was thought very difficult to kill one, except with a silver bullet, and there was a belief that the person who killed it would not live long afterwards.

Possession of the pelt of a king-otter guaranteed immunity from danger. In general, it was said that any otter, if attacked, would put his tail in his mouth and whistle, thus attracting other otters to his assistance.

PEOPLE OF THE SEA

The seals were popularly claimed to be descendants of the people left outside Noah's ark, who on rare occasions cast aside their seal-skins and danced on the shore in human shape. A story was told in some coastal areas of how a man once gained possession of the skin of a seal-woman, and while he held that she remained in human form. She married him, but on finding her skin one day, returned to the deep. This human nature attributed to seals probably derived from the human-like cry sometimes heard from these animals. Indeed, versions of the legend above bring the seal-woman nearer to human shape by calling her a mermaid.

LITTLE SUSPICIONS

The Irish stoat (*easóg*) is usually referred to in Hiberno-English as a 'weasel'. These animals are also thought to have human characteristics, organising their affairs communally and even holding funerals for their dead. To meet a weasel when setting out on a journey was a bad portent, but one could avoid the bad luck by enquiring after its health and addressing it as *a bheainín bheag uasal* (o little noble woman). Its spit was believed to be poisonous, but it was not a hostile animal unless provoked. Once, we are told, a group of haymakers accidentally destroyed a weasel's nest and, on seeing this, the mother-weasel spat in their tea-can. One of the men, however, put the young creatures in a safe place, whereupon the mother came and deliberately knocked over the can so that the men would not be poisoned.

For some reason, weasels were often said to steal coins and hoard them, and therefore it was thought that a purse made from the skin of this animal would bring wealth to its possessor. On the other hand, to take money from its nest, or otherwise to upset it, would bring bad luck. A story was told in different parts of Ireland about a man who interfered with the nest of a weasel, which came after him for revenge. In a desperate attempt to escape his pursuer, the man took ship to a foreign country, but the vengeful animal followed him on board. It traced him all the way to his new dwelling, and would have seized him by the throat while he slept had not a friend come to his assistance.

WILDEST OF ALL

Throughout most of Europe and further afield, the hare was traditionally regarded as an unlucky and even sinister creature. This idea is probably due to its nervousness and wildness, which caused man to associate it with the inse-cure and unknown side of his own nature. The Irish word for a hare (*giorria*) originally meant 'little wild one', or even 'little deer'. Because it lived in the wilderness and avoided humans, the ancient Irish regarded the deer as a strange animal which consorted with other-world beings, and they saw the hare in a similar light. Even in late folk-lore, it is said that fairies can take the form of hares, an all-white hare being especially suspect.

More disturbing notions, such as that it was unlucky to see a hare early in the morning, or that a hare lurking near the house was a sign that a member of the family was going to die, seem to have come into this country in the Middle Ages. Likewise the idea that some old women could transform themselves into the shape of a hare, which was one of the beliefs concerning witches in medieval Europe. A story is commonly told in Ireland of a farmer who noticed that the milk yield had fallen, and early one morning found a hare drinking from the cows. He attacked and wounded the hare, but it escaped, and while chasing it he came to a house where an old lady lived. He saw that she was bleeding and confronted her with this, upon which she turned back into a hare, and was killed by his dogs.

FURRY MYSTERIES

A more friendly view was held of the rabbit, as its meat was eaten and its skin used in the making of caps. Care was, however, taken in killing the animals, as dead friends and relatives were thought to return in this form on occasions to spend some time near their former dwellings.

Mice, on the other hand, ate the family food and were therefore not so welcome. They were, of course, especially busy at night, and a sore spot on the lips might be referred to as *mún luchóige* (mouse urine), in the belief that some mouse had relieved itself on the mouth of the sleeping person. On the more positive side, it was said that to eat the soup of a mouse could endow a person with the ability to see hidden treasure!

PROTECTING THE FOOD

The rat was the greatest pest in Irish life, as it ate and dirtied the grain. Accordingly, there was a wide range of superstitions deprecating it. The rat was introduced to Ireland from Norman ships in medieval times, and so, while in most areas it was called simply *luch mhór* (big mouse), in southern dialects its designation was *francach* (literally, the French one).

Folklore explained that both mice and rats originated when St Martin of Tours was salting bacon in an upturned tub. A curious woman, despite the saint's protestations, lifted the tub, and immediately the rodents raced out. Realising what a plague to humanity these creatures would be, Martin flung his glove after them, and the glove turned into a cat — hence the very first feline creature!

THE TRIUMPH OF VERSE

Since a rat's bite can be poisonous, these creatures were thought to be very vengeful and dangerous. They were also quite audacious, and one lurid tradition is that they sometimes came and drank from the breasts of sleeping women. According to a curious Irish belief, both rats and mice obey orders given to them in verse, and it was even thought that they would follow poetic instructions which were written on a piece of paper and left in a place frequented by them.

The power which Gaelic poets were said to have over rats caused some amazement to their English counterparts, and references to it are found in the works of William Shakespeare, Ben Jonson and others. Folklore records how a family whose house or barn was infested with rats would send for the local poet and have him rhyme them away. One had to be careful, however, for poets could direct the rats to go elsewhere, and a person whose pomposity or stinginess had incurred a poet's displeasure could find such a misfortune inflicted on him.

Rats were said in this way to be 'billeted' on somebody, and there were many descriptions of a mighty drove of the creatures travelling along the road under poetic orders to move from one place to another. The drove was usually led by an old decrepit rat, the senior of his clan, who would be leaning on a stick suspended between the mouths of two younger and stronger rats!

UNPLEASANT COMPANY AND
SINKING SHIPS

A rather different suggestion was that rats could bring luck to a place, provided that their numbers were kept within reason. Since these creatures are filthy and dangerous to food, and since it is very difficult completely to rid a place of them, this may have been invented in order to console people. A similar attempt to provide consolation is found in the frequent assertion that to tread accidentally in excrement is a sign of good luck.

The strong belief that the presence of rats on a ship is lucky has, however, a more realistic basis. It is well known, and often asserted as a proverb, that a vessel in danger of foundering is quickly deserted by these creatures, and so their presence on board could be taken to indicate that all was well.

FATE ON THE WING

The ancient Celts considered the raven to be a significant bird of augury, and its flight was carefully noted in the belief that the future could be divined from it. It is generally seen in negative terms. For example, the appearance of a raven while new work is being undertaken signifies that the work will not be a success; near the dwelling-house, it is taken as an omen that some member of the household will soon die. Crows are also portentous, but in their case it is thought unlucky if they leave the house or farm.

The most unlucky of all birds to see is the magpie. This belief must derive from its unusual colouring, the starkly contrasting black and white which is very noticeable and therefore felt to be unnatural. Likewise, to meet with a speckled horse — called a 'magpie pony' — is often considered a bad omen. It was thought, in fact, that the magpie was not a natural inhabitant of the Irish landscape at all, but had been brought here by Cromwell's soldiers.

A more welcome introduction, if folklore is to be credited, was the plover. This species, it was said, was introduced by the great king Brian Boru, because he

believed that such wary birds would give the alarm when
an enemy army approached the country!

A WANDERING VOICE

The cuckoo reintroduces itself into the country in late
spring of each year, and is welcomed as a harbinger of
good weather. However, some ambiguity was attached to
its call: if a person first heard it in his right ear, he would
have good fortune during the summer; but if in his left
ear, it meant the opposite. The corncrake is also
welcomed, though in recent times it has become a rarity
in Ireland. A curious item of lore regarding this bird is that
it lies on its back when calling, with its feet upwards,
thinking that in this way it keeps the sky from falling!

THOU SHALT NOT KILL

It was considered very unlucky to kill a swallow, and the
belief was that the cows' milk would become bloody as a
result. Neither should a swan be killed, for it was thought
that some swans were transformed people. This idea probably arose from the peculiar human-like cry of swans,
but also had links to the story in medieval Irish literature
of the children of the mythical King Lir, who were transformed into swans by their jealous stepmother. Although
this story did not feature much in traditional folklore,
it has become well known in recent generations
from story-books.

HEALTH, WEALTH AND WISDOM

By far the most celebrated fish is the salmon. Its high leap
has long been taken as a symbol of agility, and a favourite
wish in Irish is for 'the health of the salmon, a heart
wholesome and enduring, and to die in Ireland'. A famous
story in Irish literature and folklore tells of how Fionn
Mac Cumhaill got his great wisdom by eating a fine

salmon from the river Boyne. Fionn himself was a remarkable athlete as well as a seer, agility in mind and body being his desired object. Parents, indeed, still advise their children to eat fish before school examinations so as to clear the mind.

MINUTE FUNCTIONARIES

Because their singing behind the fireplace suggested warmth and contentment, crickets were thought to bring good fortune to a house. However, some believed that if they were suddenly heard in the dwelling, after a long silence, this was a portent of death for a member of the family. This idea may have resulted from a confusion with the death-watch beetle, the clicking of which in libraries is generally considered an omen of death. Curiously, fleas were by many people thought to be lucky in a house, keeping illness at bay since, like the leech, they extracted impurities from the blood.

LITTLE FRIENDS

The robin was held in high regard, as this bird was said to have got its red breast through its efforts to stanch the blood on the brow of Jesus on the Cross. The hedgehog was also thought to have endeavoured to help the Saviour, bringing Him an apple on its spikes after His forty days of fasting. The fact that the spider helps to control the spread of flies made it a valued insect, and this was underlined in folklore by a story that it had hidden Christ from His enemies by covering Him with its web. As a result, people believed that a spider brought luck to a house, and they would never harm it.

LITTLE FOES

For some reason, the wren was considered a cursed bird, a rather unfair belief which was also common in some other

areas of western Europe. It was said that it betrayed the
first Christian martyr, St Stephen, by beating its wings on
the drums of sleeping soldiers to alert them when Stephen
passed by as a fugitive. It was symbolically hunted on the
feast-day of the saint, a tradition which many scholars
think evolved from an ancient ritual of expelling the spirit
of winter.

Disapproval of the wren may have been compounded
by its tiny size and low flying, which led to its being imagined as a kind of disguised insect. Also, being a very fertile
little fellow, it was regarded as promiscuous, which would
not have endeared it to the more puritanical type of
Christian preacher. The upright tail of the wren accords
with the same sexual imagery, as does that of the black
chafer, which raises its tail when threatened. The chafer
(known in Irish as *daradaol* or *deargadaol*) was also given an
anti-Christian significance. It was said to have informed
on Christ — thereby leading to His capture — and to be
the only insect to enter the tomb of the dead Saviour.

REALMS OF MYSTERY

The belief in an other-world community, which shares
the environment with us but is not necessarily visible to
us, is found in many old cultures. Early Irish literature tells
of how people, after death, live on in such a world parallel
to our own, and can intermingle with human life at
special times, or when they wish to do so. These ancestors
were said, naturally, to have their residences in the burial
mounds or tumuli.

The ancient Irish word for a tumulus was *sídh*, and in
time this word was taken to refer also to the actual inhabitants of the tumuli. So, in Irish folklore, the other-world
community is referred to as the people of the *sídh* (in
modern spelling, *sí*). Due to a combination of respect and

fear, however, this word for them is usually avoided, and circumlocutions are used — such as *na daoine maithe* (the good people) and *na daoine uaisle* (the nobles). In ordinary speech, even those designations may not be used, and the members of the other-world referred to simply as 'they' and 'them'. The common term for them in English is 'the fairies', but this term is also avoided in Irish folk speech.

THE LIVING LANDSCAPE

The general tendency is for superstition to situate these spiritual beings in features of the landscape which are cultural rather than natural. In the same way as the early Irish located the Celtic deities in old burial sites — for instance, Newgrange in Co. Meath — so the folk sensed that ancient constructions were the proper place for the fairies. Throughout Ireland, there are many earthenwork forts, or 'raths' — actually the remains of early dwelling-sites. It was widely believed that these raths were inhabited by the fairies.

Medieval Irish literature explains this belief by saying that a spiritual people, known as *Tuatha Dé Danann*, were defeated in battle by our Irish ancestors, and accepted the terms of a treaty whereby they would live in underground dwellings. This, however, was learned invention. The earlier tradition must have been that both deities and the dead had their residences in sacred places. Something of this survives in the frequent folk statements that sites such as hilltop cairns are inhabited by the fairies.

THE WORLD BESIDE US

Music can sometimes be heard at night from places reputed to be fairy-dwellings, as the other-world community engages in feasting and dancing inside, and a late traveller might even see a great hurling-match being played by them in the field beside a rath. As a further reflection of human culture, the fairies were believed to farm their mystical livestock, and some stories tell of a fairy man coming to buy and sell at an ordinary market. However, any money which he handed over by way of transaction was likely to turn into withered leaves as soon as he left!

There were tales of individuals who, ignoring fairy sensibilities, levelled or dug up a rath, and met with some misfortune as a result. In a similar vein, a solitary tree standing in the middle of a field — particularly a whitethorn — was thought to be a *crann sí* (fairy tree) and to be especially dear to the fairies. If such a tree were cut down, the offender was liable soon to meet with an accident, or even death.

Old Irish literature tells of how the *Tuatha Dé* sometimes fought battles among themselves, and it is not surprising to find this idea also associated with the fairies in superstitions. Noises heard at night could be interpreted in this way, as well as prehistoric arrowheads found near raths. Milk or any other light-coloured substance seen on the ground in the morning might be interpreted as blood spilt during these battles, for fairy blood was believed to be white.

BY INVITATION ONLY
Just as the old literature describes how the *Tuatha Dé* took human heroes into their world in order to help them in their battles, so folklore describes the fairies taking good hurlers away overnight to join their teams. They also carried off accomplished musicians to provide entertainment at their feasts. The most sumptuous food was offered to the human visitor there, but if he partook of it, he would never be able to return to his worldly existence.

FINE GIFTS FROM THE BEYOND

Again like the *Tuatha Dé* of old, the fairies were believed
sometimes to bestow artistic gifts upon humans, especially
skill at music or in poetry. Many stories told of how a
great musician or poet first got his talent when he fell
asleep one night on a fairy rath. Several such artists were
blind or of poor sight in traditional Ireland, and this social
reality was explained by the assertion that they had lost
their sight after a fairy vision. Particularly in the case of a
poet, it was claimed that a beautiful fairy lady was the
donor of the gift, and the light emanating from her was so
strong that he was blinded.

CROSSING THE BRIDGE

Perhaps as a remnant of the veneration for the dead in
ancient times, and of the tradition that they lived on in a
neighbourly other-world, there was a vestige of belief that
those who died joined the fairy world. It was sometimes
said that, upon the death of a person, a door would be
heard to close in a hillside. A very popular folk legend tells
of how a young woman died, and after her burial
appeared in a dream to her husband and told him that she
would be passing with a fairy cavalcade at a certain place
and at a certain time. She instructed him to bring a black-
hafted knife, and to plunge it into the horse on which she
was riding. This would effect her escape and return to life.
When the husband met the cavalry, however, he hesitated, and so she was lost to him forever.

TO A PLACE UNKNOWN

Many people believed in fairy abduction, and especially
regarding children and mothers after childbirth, this was a
ready-to-hand explanation of unexpected and mysterious
ailments. A healthy child or young woman who suddenly

began to pine was thought to be in the process of being
taken away by the fairies.

A common European legend was imported into
Ireland some centuries ago to dramatise this belief.
According to the legend, a family friend noticed that the
appearance of a baby had changed significantly, and
discovered that the real baby had in fact been taken by
the fairies and a miserable changeling left in its place.
When he heated the tongs in the fire and threatened the
changeling with it, the latter raced from the cradle, out
the door, and into a nearby fairy rath. In a short time, the
real baby was mysteriously returned to the family, as safe
and well as ever.

LET THEM STAY

Irish lore of the *sí* has, in fact, been much influenced by
medieval notions in other European countries concerning
the fairy world. One such notion was that the fairies are
some of the angels who rebelled against God and were
expelled from Heaven as a result. After His initial wrath,
the Almighty relented somewhat and said that these angels
need not fall any lower than the point at which they then
were. So, we are told, the fairies are the angels who had
reached the level of the earth. Others had fallen into the
sea — which ties in well with the many Irish stories which
have humans being transported to other-world dwellings
across or even underneath the sea.

HILL AND HOUSE

According to a legend told of many hills in Ireland, but
especially of Slievenamon in Co. Tipperary, three fairy
women tried to abduct a woman from her house, but she
tricked them by persuading them to help her with the
spinning-wheel. She then rushed to the door and, feigning

alarm, said that the top of the hill was on fire. Fearing that their dwelling there was ablaze, the fairy women raced out of the house, and the woman slammed the door shut. She prevented them from returning by keeping the dirty washing-water in the house from that time onwards. The fairies, being very fastidious, would not go near a place where dirty water was kept.

THE LITTLE CELEBRITY

The motif of outwitting by means of a trick occurs in another very common Irish legend, though in this the tables are turned. It concerns the leprechaun, a diminutive but well-dressed little fellow sometimes claimed to be shoemaker to the fairies. He is said to have a hidden crock of gold, the whereabouts of which he will disclose if he is caught and kept within sight. According to the legend, a man caught him once and, holding him firmly in his grasp, demanded to know where the treasure was. The quick-witted leprechaun, however, shouted out that a fearsome animal was approaching the man from behind, and the man turned away to look. There was, of course, no such animal, but when the man looked back again, the leprechaun was gone!

This elusive fellow — who is generally alone when encountered — seems to derive from ideas in early European literature concerning treasure-guarding dwarves. His original name in Irish was *luchorpán*, meaning 'small-bodied fellow', and he is known by local corruptions of this in different parts of Ireland — such as *luchramán*, *clúracán*, *loimreachán*, *lurgadán* and *luchragán*, as well as *leipreachán*.

LONELY CRY AT NIGHT

The most famous of all other-world beings in Ireland is
the banshee (from the Irish *bean sí*: other-world woman).
She is a distinctively Gaelic personage, and probably
evolved from old ideas of the land-goddess as patroness of
kings and chieftains. In folk belief, her wailing cry is heard
near to the dwelling-house when a member of the family
is about to die.

This belief is still very strong in Ireland, and dwellers
in towns and cities claim to hear the banshee before a
death, just as people in rural areas do. She even seems to
keep abreast of the fortunes of the Irish all over the world,
for many claim to have heard her lamentation, without
any apparent cause, only to learn soon afterwards that a
relative had died abroad.

THE GREAT SURVIVOR

The banshee is hardly ever seen, and those people who
claim to have caught a fleeting glimpse of her are not in
agreement as to her appearance. Some say that she is a
haggard-looking little woman, while others claim that she
is a fine, fair-haired lady with a long cloak. This contrast
in appearances, in fact, parallels descriptions of the goddess
of sovereignty in old Irish literature — where the lady
Ireland is young and beautiful when the country prospers
but is old and miserable in times of misfortune.

That the banshee is a survival of ancient tradition is
further indicated by the name she is given in the folklore
of south Leinster: *badhbh* (pronounced 'bow') or *badhbh
chaointe* ('bo-heentha'). Badhbh was the name of a goddess
in early Ireland who appeared in the form of a crow and
screamed over battlefields.

FOUR

Rules and Practice of Life

S uperstitions tend to emphasise certain points in time and place, and also curious images and actions. This is a development of the natural propensity to learn, whereby striking phenomena are selected as representative of others less striking. However, the appeal of drama to human emotions means that such things are invested with a higher intensity of meaning, and accorded a particular status in superstitious thought.

LIVING IT TO THE FULL

With regard to time, intensity is attributed to special points in two basic spheres: the personal and the seasonal — that is, special points in the life of the individual person and special points in the passing of the year. In traditional understanding, the three basic points in the life of a person are birth, marriage and death, and it is not surprising that many superstitions cluster around these three.

NEW LIFE

The birth of a child was a matter of great social importance and, as both imagination and tradition will always have it, this was expressed in mystical terms. It was said in Ireland that sterility could be overcome by a couple's sleeping on top of a dolmen, the remains of an ancient burial chamber, which consisted of a fairly flat stone placed across upright ones. These dolmens are found in many parts of the country, and the common term for one was *Leaba Dhiarmada agus Ghráinne* — the bed of Diarmaid Ó Duibhne and Gráinne. It was said that the eloping lovers, in their flight from Fionn Mac Cumhaill and his men, slept in the relative safety of these raised 'beds'.

There were thought to be many external dangers to conception. For instance, if an enemy tied a knot in a handkerchief when two people were married, no child would be born to the couple until the malicious knot were opened. It was widely believed that a pregnant woman should avoid meeting a hare, for if one crossed her path, her child would be born with its most noticeable attribute, a 'hare-lip'. This could be prevented, however, if the woman tore the hem of her skirt when she saw the hare, thus transferring the blemish from the child's mouth to the clothing.

THE TIME OF TRAVAIL

A pregnant woman should not attend a wake, as it was feared that proximity to a corpse might attract death to the unborn child. This is an example of the principle, strong in folk belief, that things contiguous to each other can have an effect on each other. A pregnant woman should also avoid entering a graveyard, for if she stepped over a grave, the child would be born with a twisted foot.

Versions of the far-flung rite known as 'couvade', which consisted of an attempt by the father to take the pains of childbirth away from his wife, were known in Ireland. Thus a woman about to bear a child might wear a waistcoat or some other item of clothing belonging to her husband, in the belief that this would transfer the pains to him. Alternatively, the man might do some special type of heavy work until the birth — like digging a rough garden or drawing bucket after bucket of water from the well — in order to attract to himself the physical exhaustion. These are examples of an idea which is often at work in folk thought — that there is limited energy in the world and that this energy can only be shared, not increased or diminished.

WISH OF PARENTS

When it came to the birth itself, the importance of time was particularly stressed. A child born at night was said to have the power of seeing ghosts and fairies, and if fortunate enough to be born at the stroke of midnight, would be very intelligent, perhaps even a poet of excellence. In Ireland, as abroad, special notice was taken of a child born with a 'caul', called *caipín an tsonais* (cap of happiness), and he was thought destined to have great good fortune in life. Some people went so far as to preserve the caul for good luck or even for use in cures.

For some reason, it was considered unlucky for a child to be born on Whit Sunday, for he would grow up either to kill or to be killed. To avoid this fate, an unfortunate worm would be crushed in such a baby's hand after birth, as the destined killing was then deemed to have been done.

PAIRING OFF

Marriage was also a crucial time in human life, and there was a strong feeling in traditional Ireland that a person did not really come of age and become a full adult member of the community until he married. Many superstitions centred on the wedding ceremony. For instance, certain days of the week — such as Monday or Friday — were believed unlucky for it. Similarly, the colour green was unlucky, and should not be worn by the bride. It was also considered unlucky if it rained, if a glass or cup were broken on the morning before the wedding, if a dog licked either groom or bride, if the wedding-ring fell to the floor during the ceremony, or if somebody kissed the bride before the groom did so.

There were certain customs which were thought to bring good luck to the newly married couple — throwing something after them as they left the church, for instance, or throwing coins into the air over their heads. It was, indeed, usual for youngsters attending the wedding to gather outside the church door and tussle for the money as it fell. When the newly-weds reached their house, it was believed to bring them good luck if a man, rather than a woman, were the first to greet them, and of course the groom was supposed to carry the bride over the threshold, as a symbol of the gentility which a man should show towards his wife.

THE RACE FOR HAPPINESS

In some parts of the country, all the able-bodied men would race from the church gate, or from some other convenient point, to the house of the couple. This race might take place on horseback, in which case the men's wives would be seated behind them. This was called 'the race for the bottle', the prize usually being a bottle of whiskey on a wall near the house. Once the bride entered her new home, the mother-in-law would break a cake of bread over her head, as a token that she would henceforth be the mistress of baking and other domestic business in her new dwelling.

THE WHEEL OF SORROW

The last point of great importance is, of course, death, the supreme negative. As an old saying in Irish has it, 'There is no herb or cure for death.' Death was sometimes personified as a sombre spectrum seen lingering about the dwelling of the destined person. There were other images, such as a cloud formation looking like a funeral cortège in the sky, which presaged a death in the locality. The unavoidable reality of death was dramatised by a very old belief in Ireland, that of *fód an bháis* (the sod of death). It was fancifully claimed that a particular sod was predestined for each person, and that in this way we will all die on our own 'sods'. This, of course, was especially suitable as an explanation for a tragic or unexpected death.

In the case of fatal illness, relatives of the sick person would generally be tense, and become conscious of somewhat unusual things in the surroundings which normally might go unnoticed. These were then interpreted as portents of death: for instance, a bird perching on the window-sill, a dog howling at night, a scald-crow flying over the house, a picture which chanced to fall from the wall, or even bees leaving their hive. And, of course, any strange high-pitched sound heard outside might be taken for the cry of the banshee.

THE FINAL RESOLUTION

Care was taken to keep the household fire burning, as a weakening of it was believed to cause a diminution in the health of the patient. If a dying person felt discomfort or pain, it was often ascribed to the presence of the feather of a wild bird in the mattress, and the patient would be moved to another bed.

As the ailing person expired, doors and windows would be opened and, in olden times, a hole would be made in the thatch of the house, so as to ease the passing of the soul. Nobody present would stand or kneel between the dying person and these exits. The soul was thought to leave the body through the crown of the head, but it might linger a little in the house, and so relatives and friends refrained for a while from keening or lamenting.

NO GOING BACK

When a person died, the household clock would be stopped, mirrors turned to the wall, and any pet animals in the house put out. The origin of these customs must be some form of belief in reincarnation — that is, a fear that the soul or 'spirit' of the dead person might pass into some potential body, such as an object which moved or showed variation. After some time, the windows were closed and the curtains drawn — presumably to prevent the departed soul from returning to the house.

There was definitely a certain amount of fear of the dead in traditional folk belief. For example, roundabout ways were taken by the funeral procession to the cemetery, and in some places the coffin was carried around the graveyard a few times before burial. The origin of this custom must have been to put astray the ghost of the dead person lest it return to reassert its role in the affairs of the living. This, as with most explanations for folk customs and beliefs, has been forgotten. Indeed, it is not by rationale that folklore survives, but by repetition. Veneration grows for something which is so often performed that it becomes traditional; as the old saying in Irish goes, *Ná déan nós agus ná bris nós* (Don't make a custom and don't break a custom).

REMAINING WITH US

The most important way of all for the community to express its concern for the dead was the custom of waking: that is, keeping the body of the deceased in his own dwelling until burial. The wakes were great social occasions. Neighbours and friends congregated in the house in the evening, and stories were told, songs were sung, music and dancing took place, and many games were played to while away the night.

The dead person was not only lamented loudly in these old wakes, but often addressed as if alive. The tobacco-pipe was extended to the corpse as it was to all

the adults present, and when card-games were played it might even be given its own hand. The most plausible explanation for these strange practices is that an attempt was being made to reassure the dead person that he was not being rejected by the community, and therefore had no need to feel peeved.

JOURNEY INTO THE UNKNOWN

These notions are, of course, somewhat at variance with Christian tradition, and for that reason were often censured by the clergy. But old ideas, particularly when they are concerned with such a crucial human issue as death, themselves die hard. Other survivals of ancient traditions include the belief that one should not wear the clothes of a deceased relative for some time after his death, and the custom of leaving food on the grave for a few days after a burial. The soul, it was said, was on its way to the afterlife, travelling a long and cold road, and thus needed its clothes and sustenance.

THE SEASON OF GLOOM

The November Festival had much ancient ritual associated with the dead. Marking the beginning of the cold, wet and dark season of winter, it was a time when the living stayed indoors as much as possible. In the old literature, the eerie nature of *Oíche Shamhna* (Hallowe'en) was conveyed by accounts of cairns and other-world dwellings being open at that time, and of the adventures of ordinary folk who entered them.

The belief persists that ghosts of the dead are more likely to be encountered at Hallowe'en. Until recently, many people retired to bed early on that night, leaving food and drink on the table for their dead relatives, who it was thought might return to spend the night in the kitchen of their old houses. It was also believed that on

Hallowe'en night the spirits of the dead came from the graveyard to the local church, and spent some time praying there. Much of this lore has now become attached to the Church feast of All Souls, two days later.

THE TWO SIDES

The Irish year was basically divided into two parts, as the old saying goes, *ó Shamhain go Bealtaine is ó Bhealtaine go Samhain* (from November to May and from May to November). May, as the beginning of summer, symbolised the coming of good weather and of agricultural gain. Since folk thought tends to look upon beginnings as presaging what follows, people were anxious that all indications would be good at this time. Nobody would give any belongings away on May Eve, and anybody who asked for such was believed to be trying to steal a neighbour's good fortune. One who asked for a loan of salt, or who took lighting from the household fire, was immediately suspect.

Superstition was especially strong regarding matters which involved no certainty, such as milk, hay and crops. The dew on fields in the morning has long been a symbol of agricultural prosperity, and it was thought that greedy or malicious people might try to gather some from a neighbour's field before dawn on May Eve. Similarly, they might try to skim the top layer of water off a neighbour's well, and some farmers would stay up all night guarding their properties from such a foray.

A common legend told of a family which found that, despite all its efforts, its milk would not convert to butter on May Eve. To remedy this, the red-hot coulter of a plough was placed in the churn, and immediately a neighbour came screaming to the house, begging to be released from a terrible stomach-pain. This was the neighbour who had placed the hostile charm on the churn.

THE PROTECTIVE SAINTS

The beginnings of the other two seasons, spring and
autumn, had customs of their own attached to them.
The first day of February was anciently called *oímelg*
(which meant lactation), and introduced the season of
birth of young animals. It has long been known in Ireland
as the Feast of St Brigid, who is the special patroness of
cattle. Crosses were woven from rushes in her honour at
this time, and placed in the cattle-byre as a protection for
the animals. Also, a piece of cloth would be left outside
the house on the eve of the feast, as it was believed that
the saint passed by during the night and would bless it.
This, the *brat Bhríde* (Brigid's cloak), was afterwards
kept as a talisman.

The autumn festival celebrated the start of harvesting,
and was called *Lughnasa*, after the ancient Celtic god
Lugh. In folk tradition, it too has become Christianised,
and is said to commemorate the conversion by St Patrick
of a great apocryphal pagan called Crom Dubh. At this
time, people were in celebratory mood, climbing hilltops,
or assembling at rivers and lakes and taking part in
outdoor sports. Bilberries or whortleberries (*fraocháin*)
were picked and eaten, these being symbolic of the first
fruits of the harvest.

THE SURVIVING SPIRIT

The good farmer tried to have his harvest saved before
September. As the work neared its end, special attention
was paid to the cutting of the last sheaf. In most of the
north and of the midlands, this was called the *cailleach*
(hag), and the belief was that a hare retreated before the
mowers and took up its last hiding-place within it. It is
easy to distinguish here an original idea concerning a spirit
of the harvest.

In some places, indeed, this last sheaf was thought to have magical properties, and would be brought home and hung in the dwelling-house or barn for good luck. However, it was said that some malicious individuals could make a very special use of their own of this sheaf. They would steal it and bury it in the ground, and as it decayed, so too would the health of the rightful owner. In such a case, the only cure was for the owner to find it again and burn it.

BRIGHT AND POWERFUL

With regard to agricultural luck and prosperity, mention should also be made of the bonfires of midsummer, or St John's Night. In Ireland, as elsewhere in Europe, people assembled around these fires and danced, sang and made merry. It was customary in some parts of the country to drive the cattle between two bonfires, in the expectation that this would protect them from disease, and for young men and women to jump over the corners of the fires in order to guarantee marriage and fertility. When the bonfires had died down, their embers were scattered on the fields and haggards in the belief that this would bring about growth — a further illustration of the supernatural power often attributed to fire.

THE APPEAL OF RELIGION

The two major Church festivals, Easter and Christmas, have much lore attached to them. No nails were driven into timber on Good Friday, out of respect for Christ's death, and women would let their hair hang loose as a sign of sorrow. Since Christ's death was redemptive, it was considered a great blessing for an ailing person to depart this life on Good Friday. Also as an echo of the Gospels, it was thought that if a gale arose on this day, it would abate on Easter Sunday.

Christmas, as the day commemorating the birth of the Saviour, was of paramount importance in traditional Irish life. It was believed that the gates of Heaven were open at this time, and that anybody who died during the twelve days of Christmas had an easy passage there. On Christmas Eve itself, a special candle was lit in the window, as a symbolic guide to the Holy Family wandering the lonely roads outside as they had on the first Christmas. It was said that, in memory of the holy birth, all of creation rejoiced at midnight on Christmas Eve, and that the donkeys and cows briefly got the gift of speech to praise the divine child.

MARVELS OF THE MIND

Another imaginative tradition of high order was connected with the Epiphany, known in Ireland as Little Christmas or Women's Christmas. As the twelve days came to their conclusion, at midnight of this festival, three colourful transformations fleetingly took place — the water in the well became wine, the rushes became silk and the sandstone became gold. A human should not go out of his way to observe these marvels, however, and humorous stories were told of topers who were so audacious as to drink the transformed water and were turned into stone as a result!

TIMES GOOD AND BAD

The unluckiest date, according to Irish superstition, was 28 December, when the slaughter of the Holy Innocents was commemorated. This was known as 'the forbidden day of the year', and no new enterprise was undertaken upon it. Conversely, New Year's Day was a good date for starting a task, as it was felt to cast its influence on all of the year that followed it.

A NEW BEGINNING

In former times, it was customary for the family to have a big meal on New Year's Eve, and to throw a cake against the kitchen door so as to banish hunger. On New Year's Day itself, special notice was taken of the weather, as this was thought to betoken the general trend during the ensuing year. Some people even thought that the economic prospects could be ascertained by placing a stick in the river: if the water-level fell, it was welcomed as an indication of a decrease in prices; if it rose, inflation was in store!

Many things seen or experienced in the New Year were taken to presage the future. For instance, if the first horse seen by a person had its head towards him, that was a sign of good luck, but its rear meant bad luck. To find a horseshoe on the road augured well for the year, but it had to be turned towards the person in order to channel the good fortune in his direction. Similarly, it was considered auspicious to discover a pin on the road on one's first trip outdoors on New Year's Day, provided also that it is pointing towards the observer.

THE DAY OF REST

Note was taken of the days of the week, and particular traits associated with them. Sunday was in many ways the most important. Since Church rules forbade unnecessary servile work on this day, it was believed that work carried out was unlucky and always proved futile. Furthermore, people should not work too near to the junctures — *buille déanach an tSathairn agus buille luath an Luain* (the late stroke on Saturday and the early stroke on Monday) must be avoided. If absolutely necessary, a woman might put a stitch in a garment on Sunday, but she would be careful to replace it with a new stitch on the following day.

Children born on Sunday were expected to be of a
saintly disposition. Herbs picked then were said to be
more effective in curing ailments, and it was thought that
the fairies could not overhear human conversation on the
Lord's Day. On a more mundane level, since it is the first
day of the week, many farmers thought it a good day on
which to change the cattle from one pasture to another.

ONE DAY AT A TIME

For some reason, Monday was thought unsuitable for any
new undertaking. If a field had to be ploughed on that
day, the first sod would be turned on the preceding
Saturday, and if a grave had to be dug, one sod would be
cut on the Sunday. It was believed inadvisable to part with
money on that day — in fact, people even avoided
sweeping the dust out of the house on a Monday, for fear
they would be giving their good luck away!

Tuesday, on the other hand, was a good day to begin
a job, and was strongly recommended for churning butter
or for any type of spinning. Many people considered it the
luckiest day of the week, and it was an especially popular
one for weddings — probably because of the importance
of Shrove Tuesday as the last day before Lent on which a
marriage would be solemnised.

THINGS REPEATED

Wednesday was regarded as the best day for buying and
selling, and also for moving house or for travel. Seafarers,
indeed, placed great trust in this day, as it was thought
usually to presage a change for the better in the weather;
the old saying was, *Ní théann stoirm thar Dhomhnach ná
rabharta thar Chéadaoin* (A storm does not last longer than
Sunday nor a swell longer than Wednesday). There was

one notable exception to this good fortune, namely Spy
Wednesday, which was considered a most unlucky day
because of its commemoration of the betrayal of Christ.

A TIME FOR HEALING

Thursday was also a good day for markets and for any
other kind of commercial transaction, but its particular
importance lay in the realm of curing illnesses. People
preferred this day for visits to the local doctor or healer,
and in a similar vein, many made a habit of washing and
shaving on Thursday. There may be echoes in all of this of
Christ's celebration of the Last Supper and institution of
the Eucharist.

Because of the Crucifixion, Friday was a day on
which it was thought that people should take special care
at their prayers. It was also considered a very good day for
starting new work — but never for marrying, as this
would be too joyful and festive an event. Since there was
an association between Friday and storms, people were
loth to go to sea on that day.

THE WEEKEND BREAK

Coming at the end of a hard week's work, Saturday found
people in good spirits, and it was said that the sun would
never fail to shine then, at least for a brief period. In many
areas, indeed, it was regarded as a day especially devoted
to the Blessed Virgin. The injunction has it thus, *Fág an
Satharn ag Muire Mháthair!* (Leave the Saturday to Mother
Mary!) Accordingly, it was a sort of second day of rest
and, although housework and other necessary chores
were recommended, large undertakings like the beginning
of house-building or the launch of a new boat were
considered unlucky.

COUNTING WITH CARE

The week is a cultural rather than a natural unit of time, and its importance in the folk mind is in large part due to its division into seven days. Particular importance is attributed to the number seven in many cultures. In Ireland, several preternatural occurrences — such as visions of fairy dwellings — were said to take place every seven years.

Children were said first to show their individual abilities at the age of seven, and on the darker side, a curse on a family was believed to run for seven generations. The seventh son of a seventh son was thought to have extraordinary healing powers, probably due to the rareness of such a person in the community. Likewise, a posthumous child — also comparatively rare — was said to have the gift of healing.

HOW MANY TIMES?

Of the other numbers, three was the most important in Ireland. This is a very old belief, for the early literature refers to several Celtic deities who were triplicate. Major events in folk stories often occur three times, and triads figure prominently in Irish proverbs. This number has connotations of roundness and totality, and many ritual acts — such as walking around a bonfire on St John's Night or doing rounds at a holy well — were performed thrice. If one dreamed of the same thing on three nights running, this was taken as proof that the dream was true.

MYSTERY AND SILENCE

Hidden treasures of the personality, like the know-how of healing, were usually kept secret, a tradition reinforced by the belief that such a gift, if divulged, would desert its possessor. Similarly, it was held that secrets concerning the private affairs of others should be kept, misfortune befalling the person who broke this rule. No small effort might be involved in thus keeping good faith, for it was thought that a secret could cause its possessor great stress and even failure of health. To avoid this, he might confide it to an innocent witness, such as an animal, tree, stone, or hole in the wall.

CHOOSING WORDS CAREFULLY

The ideal of mutual dependence has always been a mark of Irish life, and this is reflected in beliefs concerning the use of speech. Some words could cause harm, even if uttered without bad intent. For instance, one should not carelessly say, 'God bless the work' to those digging a grave, nor should one welcome a neighbour to a wake. And nobody should ever utter an oath such as 'May I die if this is not true!'

When wishing for good fortune, a person should be as inclusive as possible, for the *guí ghann* (stingy prayer) could cause ill luck to befall those for whom it was made. The idea was that such a wish contained an element of jealousy. A person who scoffed at the handicap of another, or who compared the traits of a fellow to those of an animal, was thought to be inviting harm onto himself. Similarly, mimicry was frowned upon, and thought potentially dangerous to those who engaged in it, for as the saying goes, 'Mocking is catching.'

A curious belief concerning *uair na hachainí* (the time of wishing) claimed that there was a certain time in each day at which, if one expressed a wish, it would be granted. A story was told about an old woman who, seeking to avail of this, prayed continuously one day that her son would become King of Ireland. During her prayers, a large lump of soot fell from the chimney into the fireplace,

and she exclaimed, 'Blast you, chimney!' It immediately
took fire, almost destroying the house, and she barely
escaped with her life.

RESOURCES OF THE ENVIRONMENT

Many objects were believed to bring good luck and to
banish misfortune. Iron was, in Ireland as abroad, believed
to be especially powerful in this regard, and because he
worked with iron, the blacksmith was considered a wise
counsellor with powers of healing. He could banish
ailments, and even spirits, by pointing a piece of red-hot
iron in their direction, or by turning the anvil towards
them. Water used for cooling iron in the forge was
thought to have properties of healing, especially in the
case of warts. Another type of water much in demand was
that blessed in the church at Easter — people would
sprinkle this on the boundaries of their properties to
protect their good fortune.

Some emphasis was placed on directions. For instance,
to sleep facing eastwards invited death, as graves were
usually in that position. To sleep facing northwards
ensured good health, presumably because it might accli-
matise one to the harsh weather which the north wind
represented. No doubt because of its association with the
sun, it was thought lucky to change residence southwards,
except on Mondays or Fridays. The west, representing
the sunset, was usually associated with decline, and it was
considered proper that the room furthest west in the
house should be occupied by the oldest member of
the family.

Junctures in space, as those in time, were given special
importance in folk thought. To enter a new part of the
landscape, indeed, could easily be assimilated to the experience of entering a new stage of one's life. Crossroads and

bridges were accordingly thought to be places where either good or bad fortune might be encountered. Several stories told of people who met with ghosts at such locations, but the landscape also offered remedies to such predicaments, for it was commonly held that spirits could not cross running water or a boundary between two townlands.

POWER UNBROKEN

The belief that lines enclosed power was especially strong in the case of a circle, the symbol of totality. A healer treating a skin ailment would often draw a circle around it in red ink, claiming that the malfunction would be confined within that area. Similarly, a gold ring was applied to the eye to cure a sty or to the tooth to ease toothache. It was sometimes said that if one looked through such a ring the fairies could be seen, for a gold ring, being small and colourful, was felt to have a kind of microscopic effect and so provide a window onto the flitting spiritual world. Fanciful as they are, superstitions entail a large degree not only of calculation but of silhouetting, which accounts for the strong visual sense lying behind many of them.

THE ARTIST WITHIN

People would often argue at length over whether meeting with a black cat indicated good or bad luck. However, while the interpretation was not definitive, the image was a constant, the striking mental picture of an animal so black as to stand out vividly from its surroundings. The part played by colour in superstition seems to be at all times connected with the 'visual' sharpening of the imagination.

This is further illustrated by superstitions concerning the colour red. This colour was, on the one hand, taken to be a bad omen in the case of a fox or a red-haired woman encountered before going on the sea, but had a positive function when a red ribbon was attached to a child or a farm animal in order to repel illness or to prevent damage by the evil eye. White too had long associations with the other-world, and had equally ambiguous power. A white cow, for instance, was said to bring bad luck to a herd, but dressing children in white clothes was thought to protect them from being taken into the fairy world.

In paying tribute to this 'aesthetic' tendency in superstition, we conclude by citing the three unluckiest things to gaze upon early in the morning: 'a white horse, a house on a height and a fine woman'. Noting the fact that these rhyme (*capall bán, tigh ar ard agus bean bhreá*), we may doubt the negative interpretation, and instead appreciate the attractive imagery of all three against the background of a dull and dreary daybreak.

IRISH FAIRY TALES

PADRAIC O'FARRELL

To Siofra

Contents

Introduction

Are they the Tuatha Dé Danaan, those tribes of the Celtic goddess, Dana, who retired into the hills of Ireland after their defeat by the Milesians? Are they servants of the gods? Are they the angelic hurlers on the ditch who took neither side in the struggle between the Archangel and Lucifer and who, as a result, must wander this world until the Day of Judgment? Are they evil or good? Do they live in communities or operate alone? In the Land of Youth, Tír na n-Óg, or in ordinary fairy mounds called *liosacháin*. Are they merely devices used by the *seanchaí*, that popular Irish story-teller given to entertaining his neighbours by the fireside with his well-embellished tales? Whatever their origin, the *sidhe*, the good people, the wee folk, the fairies, fill pages of Irish literature as well as enriching a wealth of oral tradition.

Irish scholars have chronicled fairy tales for centuries. Monks in ancient abbeys used stylish calligraphy and artistic diagrams to develop themes of great quests in the Eastern world or hostings in the hearts of Irish hills. Authors like William Carleton, Lady Wilde, W. B. Yeats and Lady Gregory contributed to this corpus. The Kerry playwright, George Fitzmaurice, crammed *The Enchanted Land* with inhabitants of the sea-bed land of Manannan Mac Lir, an Irish version of the sea-god, Neptune. The waves and their wildlife — seals and fish, mermaids and phantom craft — have associations with fairies too. Music and dancing and merriment abounded in some fairy tales. So did feats of horsemanship and of strength, alongside weaknesses, wiles and wantonness. Seldom did the written word equal the effect of the oral narrative. It did, however, present the *seanchaí* with a basic pattern upon which to weave his descriptive tapestry. And how he revelled in his art of embellishment and exaggeration! As one generation passed on its fanciful tales to the next, the basic story remained the same but an added charm came with each retelling.

Country people steeped in superstition sometimes feared the *sidhe.* More often, they enjoyed listening to stories about them. Many doubters played practical jokes on believers. However they might scoff at the same believers, they held in their hearts an acceptance of the possibility of a supernatural existence in the form of fairies. Some families swore that the Banshee (*Bean sidhe,* fairy woman) keened on the night before the death of a member. Others would never build a house between two fairy forts, because the wee folk would be passing that way. When there was a doubt about the fairies' right of way, builders left foundations unfilled for a few nights; if the trenches crossed a fairy pass, the wee folk would fill them in and the builder would choose another site. A returned American defied custom and built on a fairy pass, against all local advice. He held a house warming, a party to celebrate the occupation of the newly built premises. Good spirits prevailed until midnight when bad spirits had their fling in earnest. They flung pots, pans, kettles and assorted earthenware around the house. Then the roof fell in. As revellers scattered, they were buffeted by an unknown force. The piper stopped playing when his mouth went around to the back of his head. A horn protruded from the owner's forehead. By morning, nothing remained of the building. Next day, the owner hurried back to America. Quite recently, a land reclamation scheme ground to a halt as a JCB operator refused to tamper with a fairy fort.

A religious race mingled religion with *piseoga* (superstitious practices) and uttered an apology or exhortation to the sidhe as often as a prayer to God. Parishes had their *bean feasa* (wise woman) or *fear feasa* (wise man). Many of these received their healing powers, it was thought, from the fairies. Only a hundred years ago, a Tipperary farmer burned his young wife to death, believing that the fairies substituted her for the girl he married. Fairies could do good or evil, depending on how mortals treated them.

The Irish spirit of fun nurtured its fairy lore too. Few could deny the foreigner his pleasure of believing that around the next turn of the road might be lurking a leprechaun who would lead him to a crock of gold at the rainbow's end. If they did not, however, they frightened the life out of the same visitor with tall tales of giants and pookas that they would surely meet before their vacation ended. Or about An Fear Gurtha, the hungry man who might cast his hungry grass under their feet and lead them astray on the next leg of their journey. Lonely poets might hear about the Leannán Sidhe, the fairy lover who would seduce them in return for inspiration. (Does modern poetry testify to its extinction?) Perhaps professional babysitters eager to attract business spread the news about the little red man, An Fear Dearg, who stole healthy mortal babies and left sick fairy infants in their place.

Time passed and customs changed. A box in the corner replaced the *seanchaí*. An alleged sophistication spurned simple entertainment. So the great tradition of passing down fairy stories orally is in decline, if not completely extinct. There is, therefore, a need for

concise collections of lesser-known tales, told with a
contemporary idiom. For example, many of the best-
loved stories each took a half-hour or more to tell.
If the narrator noticed special interest in some part of his
account, he exploited this by dwelling longer on that
portion of his story with the next telling. If he had a really
rapt audience, his tale could go on for an hour. There was
considerable repetition in these stories. Invariably, a young
man seeking the hand of a princess in marriage got three
tasks to perform. The blueprint story meticulously
described identical circumstances for each attempt. The
hurly-burly world of sound-bite and Internet surfing that
heralds the approach of the twenty-first century would
not tolerate that technique.

A pocket edition demands extra brevity. This,
however, might prove to be a blessing, because I believe
that the very survival of the fairy story demands a more
fluid and brief narration than it received previously. I read
some of the stories in this collection during my lifetime.
I listened to others, sitting by country firesides in many
counties of Ireland over half a century, as a child eager for
diversion and as an adult researching books on Irish life
and lore. I do not retell them here exactly as I read or
heard them. Such a narration would not suit the time or
the medium. For the reasons stated, I write condensed
versions. Like the *seanchaí* of old, however, I have taken
the liberty of spicing the original with a little humour,
again, with a contemporary readership in mind. I hope the
wee folk will understand and permit publication!

ONE

Maureen's Cluricaun

In fairy lore, the Cluricaun is a sprite that uses a *buachalán buidhe*, or ragwort, as a steed to get him from one wealthy gentleman's house to the next or from one foxhunting meet to the other. Other branches of the *sidhe* frown upon this habit of hobnobbing with the gentry. Yet they tolerate him, because fairies admire skills in horsemanship and one who can ride a mere weed to overcome the opposition of well-bred pookas and hacks is indeed special. Such a person gains the respect of Fionvara himself, that champion huntsman, with his black stallion whose deep red nostrils breathe fire.

A Roscommon Cluricaun cantered by the shores of Lough Ree on his *buachalán* one fine summer day. He heard the horn of the master of the Galway Blazers who were far from home and searching a covert near by. Hastily, he jumped behind a furze bush and hid until the brightly clad gentry came by. As they did, he joined them. Now, to mere mortals, the Cluricaun and his mount appear as a handsome male on a fine black horse. Ladies sitting side-saddle were known to abandon decorum, throw their leg astride their hunter and gallop off in pursuit of Cluricauns, much to the chagrin of their escorts. So it was, that when the Roscommon fairy gave chase to the risen fox, he in turn was pursued by one of the fairest damsels in all the baronies of Connaught. Maureen Lahy was her name and her father was a respected landowner in the district. This ravishing beauty had hair as dark as a moonless night, skin as smooth as a peach from the East and lips as red as

holly-berry. All the men of the West adored her and
sought her favours.

The Cluricaun noticed his pursuer and swerved away
from the pack, crossing a fairy rath as he did so. Maureen
followed, but when her horse came to the rath it stopped
suddenly, throwing her over its neck. The Cluricaun
returned, dismounted and helped her to her feet. By this
time the rest of the hunt had disappeared. The stranger
amazed Maureen, because although she had never seen
him before, he asked her about her family and friends by
name. There was to be a hunt ball in Lahy's that evening,
so Maureen invited the Cluricaun to be her guest and he
gladly accepted. In return, he urged her to enter her horse
for the main event at the Knockcroghery point-to-point
race-meeting next day. He promised to provide a jockey
that would win the race for her. Maureen smiled at this,
because her nag was as slow as a wet week. She did as she
was told, however, and next morning, when she went to
the stable to saddle up her horse, a small man was standing
in the corner all dressed up in jockey's clothes. These
seemed to emit a faint amber light that had a peculiar,
soothing effect on Maureen.

'I will take over now,' the small man said, hopping up
on the horse's back and trotting off through the stable yard
and on through the fields. Maureen joined her family in
their coach and four, and soon they all reached the point-
to-point venue. There was no sign of Maureen's horse and
as the time approached for the race in which he was
entered, she grew anxious. Ten fine beasts lined up for the
start and the steward called for Little Peepers, Maureen's
entry. From behind a tree-covered hillock came her horse
and when the crowd saw the tiny rider they laughed
loudly. Maureen's father became angry and chastised his

daughter, but she told him to stay quiet and bet any
money he had on Little Peepers.

'But that horse never came anywhere but last in a
race,' he argued. Maureen knew this was so, and she
wondered why she had given her father such foolish
advice. Guided by some strange urge, Mr Lahy laid a large
bet just before the race began. As soon as the flag dropped,
a wind whistled loudly through the trees surrounding the
field and seemed to bear Little Peepers and his rider across
the highest ditches quite effortlessly. The other entries
were no match for Maureen's horse and there was great
jubilation as it finished three fields ahead of its rivals.
Maureen ran to thank the little rider, but he had
disappeared and the Cluricaun was holding the horse's
halter when she arrived at the finish.

'Where is the wonderful jockey?' she asked.

'He's gone to help prepare the reception to celebrate
our win. Come, I will lead you to it,' the Cluricaun
answered.

Maureen had lived a sheltered life. Her mother always
warned her to be wary of strange men. Now, however,
accepting the invitation seemed the most natural thing in
the world to do. The Cluricaun hoisted her on to his own
horse, then urged it on and Maureen felt as though she
were flying across a misty, light blue world of delicate
flowers and gentle breezes. They came to a mansion made
of a bright orange material and a dozen ladies-in-waiting
danced down the steps, took her to a magnificent
amethyst-tiled bathing area and gently washed her in pink
water scented with aromatic oils. Then they dressed her in
a magnificent ball gown of red and black and led her to
the dining room. Its opulence was beyond description.
Rich tapestries covered the walls and gold chandeliers

hung from the ceiling. Fifty tables sagged under the weight of fine foods and wine. She ate, drank and then danced with handsome young men.

At midnight the Cluricaun asked her to dance. When he placed his right hand around her waist, she felt a peculiar burning sensation and slowly the joy she had been experiencing gave way to fear. The Cluricaun's dark eyes seemed to turn red and his nostrils flared wickedly. Among the dancers, she noticed relatives and friends of hers that had died, some many, many years before. All seemed to have vacant, expressionless eyes; all but the man with whom she danced. The music grew louder and its beat quickened. The Cluricaun whirled her around and around the floor and his hand seemed to burn her back more and more. As it did, her feet left the floor, and now they danced through a dark night sky full of bleeding stars. A purple moon shed an eerie light but it was enough for Maureen to spot her home below. This was the first time she had thought of her parents since the race-meeting and as soon as she did, she began to say a prayer for them. Only one word and one syllable of the Our Father had escaped her lips when the Cluricaun began to scream. He whipped his hand from her waist and shook and waved it about as if it was causing him great pain. He grasped it with his left hand, letting Maureen go completely. She fell, but floated downwards gently. Six rust-coloured eagles appeared, spreading their wings beneath her and conveyed her back to her own back door. Her parents welcomed her and told her she was foolish to walk home.

'You need not have been afraid of me,' said her father. 'The horse I intended to back did not win either. And sure second-last is an improvement for Little Peepers.'

Maureen Lahy kept her counsel and forgot about her adventure until the following Easter when her dressmaker was measuring her for a new gown. She remarked on the red, hand-shaped scar on Maureen's lower back.

TWO

The Maid of Aran

The name Síofra means a fairy or fairy child. Late one autumn evening, a young Aran Island girl of that name was going to a well on Inisheer for water. She heard a bell in her ear and knew that this was the call of a soul in purgatory, a plea for prayers begging its release into the happiness of heaven. The girl murmured her Hail Marys until her foot slipped on the wet surface near the well and she fell. She felt that some evil force was objecting to her prayers. When she stood up, she could not recognise the land around her. There were no familiar trees or bushes and the well had disappeared. It was night-time, yet she could observe everything. On a hill that she

had never seen before, a huge fire blazed and a host of people were gathered around it. They were small, the tallest of them scarcely two feet high. As she walked towards them she could feel herself shrinking, and by the time she reached them, she too was tiny. Nobody smiled and the womenfolk cast furtive glances her way.

Suddenly the crowd parted and a handsome prince strode forward. To Síofra, it looked as if he had emerged from the flames. His long, fair hair glistened in the fire's glow and the clasp that tied it back was of gold. He wore a white cloak and fine brooches of silver and diamonds decorated his sash of crimson. To Síofra's amazement he approached her and asked her to dance. A little shy and very afraid, she muttered an excuse about there being no music. When she did, the prince waved his hand and a beam of light flashed from a huge ring on his finger. Instantly Síofra heard the most haunting music, as if it came from hundreds of stringed instruments. It was above and below her, to her left and to her right, and the prince took her in his arms and they began to dance. It was not the traditional Irish music to which Síofra normally listened, yet she was able to match her partner's every step. The others were dancing too but Síofra did not notice anybody but her prince. She gazed into his eyes and he returned her smile. They danced on and on until the moon sank behind the hill and the stars faded in the sky, yet the experience seemed to last only a few moments.

The music stopped and Síofra saw for the first time a long flight of marble steps leading down under the hill. The prince took her hand and led her to these. Everybody else followed. They arrived in a splendid banqueting hall, lit by dozens of golden sconces that seemed to emit a beautiful fragrance. Fine linen cloths covered the tables, and garlands of delicate flowers decorated them. Síofra had never seen such a sight. Liveried male servants bore silver dishes of fine food and shapely maidens in light gossamer dresses stood by, ready to serve wine into golden meidirs, the traditional regal drinking cups of Irish chieftains. As soon as they sat, the prince called for wine and offered it to Síofra. As he did, one of the male servants leaned over her and placed some veal on her plate. He also whispered in her ear: 'If you eat or drink in this place, you will never return to Inisheer again.'

She looked to see if she recognised the man, but by the time she raised her eyes, he was at the other end of the vast hall. She heeded his warning and refused the meidir that the prince still held out to her. His countenance darkened but he feigned a smile as he said, 'Food then? Come, you must be hungry after so much dancing.' She politely refused, and immediately there was a stillness in the hall as everybody stared sullenly at her. One swarthy, dark man approached her, calling, 'You have come to our land and have danced with our prince. How dare you insult us by refusing our hospitality!'

'Disgraceful!' 'Shame!' Murmurs of disapproval arose from the assembly and Síofra began to tremble with fear. The dark man seized the prince's cup and tried to force Síofra to drink from it. She felt his rough fingers dig into her shoulder, causing her excruciating pain and dizziness. Suddenly, the servant who had warned her earlier appeared at her side, seized her by the hand and led her away from the table. The crowd jumped up, admonishing him and uttering threats on himself and on his kinsfolk. From beneath his waistband he took a tiny muslin bag of eidhneán nimhe, poisoned ivy used by ancient Egyptians for protection against evil spirits. 'Keep this in your hand until you reach home and say your prayers somewhere else besides near the well in future,' he advised, before leaving her at the bottom of the marble steps.

She began to climb and the host of fairy folk tore the sconces from the walls and sped off in pursuit. The steps became steeper and steeper and the walls began to close in on her. Tired and exhausted, she reached the top and had just stepped out of the hill when the gap closed behind her. She was back beside the well. From its depths she heard howling and screaming from voices raised in great anger. She filled her bucket and ran home. Her mother remarked that she was back very quickly. This puzzled Síofra. When the old lady began to poke the fire, she did not seem to hear what terrified her daughter — the voice of the dark fairy. 'The fairy folk will catch you without the sachet of ivy someday and you will not escape so easily.'

Síofra sewed the talisman into her cloak, however, and never went to the well again without it. There was one strange outcome from the episode: instead of bells in her ears thereafter, Síofra heard the music that she had danced to the night she joined in the festivities of the fairy folk. When she did, she still prayed for the souls in purgatory — as long as she was not too near the well.

THREE

The Hunchback and the Mean Woman

I reland's skinflints have come to realise that there is
nothing the fairies dislike more than meanness,
especially among folk who are not without a shilling.
There lived in the hills of Donegal one time a woman
who seldom gave alms. If she did, it was only what she
had no use for. Foolishly, she thought that such charity
would enhance her chances of salvation in the next life.
Down the winding lane that led to her house came a
travelling man, one day. He was a hunchback. He asked
the woman's servant for the loan of a saucepan to boil
himself an egg. The servant asked the woman if she
could lend him one and she said, 'Of course you can.'

As the girl was taking one down from its hook,
however, the woman stopped her. She said, 'Don't give
him that one, you óinseach [foolish woman]. Hand him
out the one with the hole in it and he will have to mend
it before he boils his egg. That will save me paying
another tinker sixpence for mending it.' The servant
obeyed and, sure enough, back came the hunchback
with a perfectly mended saucepan. The mean woman
was delighted at her own craftiness. Only until supper-
time that evening, let it be said.

The servant began to boil milk for the woman's
children, who shouted at her to hurry up and pour it
over their bread pieces for their nightly 'goody'. The
contents of the saucepan foamed up and burnt and the
smell of it wafted into the next room where the woman
of the house sat eating fine food and drinking vintage
wine.

'What's going on out there?' she called, dropping her knife and fork and making for the kitchen.

'The milk burnt up as fast as a match in hell, mam.'

'You useless thing! Why didn't you watch it? Such a dreadful waste of two pints of milk!' After this admonition, the mistress jumped when she heard a voice in the chimney calling, 'That will be two pence.' It was an eerie, low monotone.

The woman herself poured a quart of milk, tried to boil it, and the same thing happened.

'That pan must be dirty,' she said, examining it. 'My goodness, four pints of milk gone to waste!'

'That will be four pence,' said the voice in the chimney.

The woman made the servant scour the saucepan before trying again. Two more pints burned up and the woman was in tears at the waste. 'Six pints of milk gone on me! What will I do at all?'

This time the voice in the chimney was jeering. 'Never again try to save paying a tinker a tanner,' it echoed, and immediately a cloud of soot filled the kitchen as down tumbled the hunchback who had borrowed the saucepan. The woman and the maid screamed as the black form almost knocked them down before running out the back door, laughing loudly.

The woman became quite decent after that and as soon as she did, the saucepan never again boiled over, even when left far too long on the fire.

FOUR

The Leprechaun and the Dandelion

On Lady's Day, thousands of people visited Tobar Muire (Mary's Well), near Dundalk. They crept around the well on their knees, nine times in a westerly direction. This, they believed, would cure all their ills and make amends for their sins. Then they would go away and begin cutting their corn. A man called Jack Fox completed the ritual and was heading for his fine field of oats with his scythe on his back. From the hedgerow, he heard a sound like the chirp of a cricket. He wondered if it was a hoarse chaffinch, but it was not the time of the year for their song. On he walked and then he heard it again. This time it sounded more urgent. Tic-tac-too, tic-tac-too. Slowly, a possibility began to dawn on Jack and, as it did, the hair on the back of his neck stood on end.

He rose on to his toes and peeped across. Nothing. Not even the sound he had been hearing. Jack walked along further and as soon as he heard the tic-tac-too again he pulled the bushes aside and looked through. A small man sat by a last, no bigger than a farthing, shaping a tiny shoe that shone like gold. The hammer with which he worked was the size of a pin. As he tapped, a pointed cap waved backwards and forwards, almost mesmerising Jack, but not enough to divert his attention from the little shoe-maker. Jack knew he was looking at a leprechaun and he remembered hearing from his mother that the rascal could lead him to a pot of gold if he made sure to keep watching him. He laid his scythe against the hedge and crept closer.

'*Bail ó Dhía ar an obair*,' ventured Jack and quickly added, 'God bless the work,' in case the leprechaun did not know Irish.

'*Go raibh maith agat*, and thank you too,' the cobbler answered, smiling. 'It's a hot day. Maybe you'd like a drink?' He reached for a pitcher that lay beside his stool. He hoped Jack would look towards the vessel but was disappointed. Jack fixed his gaze more steadily.

'What kind of drink have you?' he asked.

'*Uisce beatha*, best of gorse whiskey.'

'There's no such thing as whiskey made from gorse. Mead, perhaps, but not whiskey.'

'Taste it then, if you don't believe me,' said the leprechaun. 'Reach down there in the hedge and fetch me a glass.' Again, Jack resisted the temptation to look elsewhere.

The leprechaun tried all sorts of ruses. He told Jack that his cattle were breaking out of the field behind him. He shouted, 'Watch out. Your scythe is falling across your neck!' He told him he had heather beer as well as whiskey and that if he tasted it he would live for ever. 'The recipe is in my family for generations. The Milesians brought it over to Ireland and gave it to us.'

'And what might your name be?' Jack asked.

'Night and day and far away.'

'That's a funny name.'

'So is yours, Jack Fox. Do you live in a covert up on the Cooley Mountains or what?' the leprechaun teased.

'How do you know my name?'

'Why wouldn't I know it and I living on your farm for years.'

Jack thought it was about time he made an approach about the cobbler's crock of gold. 'Bring me to the end of the rainbow where your pot of money lies,' he ordered.

The leprechaun laughed. 'God bless us and save us, have you heard that nonsense too?'

'Come on now. No more of your old chat. Bring me there.' Jack grimaced as crossly as he could and the little man began to looked frightened. Jack could see that he was still stalling, so he issued the threat that custom demanded for such obstinacy. 'I will bring you home and roast you on the griddle.'

'I'll tell you where my crock of gold is, Jack, but it's not at the end of the rainbow. Come on.' He made to run ahead, but Jack suddenly grasped him in his hand and held him right up against his eyes for fear of being distracted. Whether he crossed a stile or climbed a bank, stumbled in rushes or leapt a stream, Jack kept his eyes glued on the back of the leprechaun's head. The fairy man led him through four small fields and into a huge, fifty acre one that was filled with dandelions. 'There you are now,' he said, pointing to one plant. 'Dig down deep under that *caisearbhán* and you will find the pot of gold. But I have to go now or the fairies will have no shoes for their big ball tonight and they will take revenge on you if that happens.'

Jack realised that he had no spade to do as he was bid. He could not even mark the spot by cutting a few dandelions near by, because he had left his scythe on the hedge where he found the leprechaun. 'Swear on your oath that the crock of gold is under that dandelion,' he ordered.

'I swear on my oath and on the oaths of all my Milesian ancestors [the last invaders of Ireland before the historical period].'

'Very well,' Jack said, 'you may go now and thanks very much. *Slán*!'

'*Slán is beannacht*, health and a blessing,' said the leprechaun, and Jack thought he noticed a glint in his eye.

Jack took off his stocking and placed it over the dandelion so that he would recognise it again. Then he walked back to his home for a spade. He told his wife about their good fortune and said it was the luckiest Lady's Day they ever had. He promised her a new house and barn and all the finery she could ever dream of. Back he went, whistling, towards the big field. When he crossed the stile into it, he screamed in anger. Over every dandelion in the fifty acres there was a stocking the same colour as his own.

'*Ochón, ochón*, woe is me,' he wailed. 'I could be digging for the rest of my life and might not be under the right dandelion. The rogue of a leprechaun has fooled me indeed.'

A flurry of wind rose from behind him and blew across the expanse of stockings. They fluttered the exact way the leprechaun's hat had done when Jack first saw him working at his last. Jack swore he could hear the hundreds of dandelions laughing. Dejected and downcast, he returned home and told his wife his sad tale.

'Well,' she said, 'there's one consolation. I'll never have to knit you another stocking.'

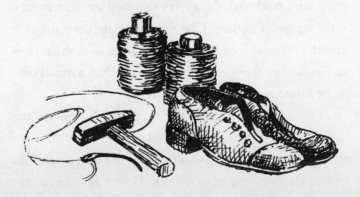

FIVE

The 'Rale Old Moll Anthony' of Kildare

D oes a pair of tombstones in the cemetery at Milltown, County Kildare, conceal some dark secret? Certainly, some people of the area are reluctant to talk about the stones. Others will not even tell of their whereabouts. The Death Register kept by the Eastern Health Board dates back to 1868 — not far enough in time to clinch an argument about one of Leinster's most famous women, Moll Anthony.

Most practitioners in the art of curing confined their cases to ailments of humans, but 'the rale old Moll Anthony of the Red Hills' seems to have had a veterinarian degree also. More, she did not always attend at the farms of the sick beasts. Once the animal's owner came to Moll, the beast was cured at the moment of consultation.

Moll did not live at the Red Hills at all but at the Hill of Grange between Milltown and Rathangan, a likely abode, this, for a woman regarded by some as being in league with the fairies, because this rise, the Hill of Allen and Donadea's Green Hill lie in a straight line. The line was a fairy track and if a wayfarer crossed any stile along it at the stroke of midnight, he would remain there for a month with one foot planted on either side of the stile — and in Kildare these contraptions always had a strand of barbed wire across the top. Precarious!

One of the many stories involving Moll Anthony tells how a boy once met a funeral and, as was the custom in times past, he turned to walk some of the way behind the coffin. He even helped to carry it. When the funeral came

back to the lad's own gate the pallbearers left down the
coffin. The boy ran in to tell his mother and when they
both came back out the coffin was still there but the
mourners had disappeared. They unscrewed the lid and a
lovely young girl of about 12 stepped from within. She
did not know who she was or from where she had come.
The family adopted her and she lived happily with them,
taking the mother's name, Mary. When she and the boy,
James, grew up, they married.

One day, the young wife asked James to bring her
with him to the fair in Castledermot. He was delighted
to have her as company and so the pair set off, intent on
having a good time. James had two cows to sell. They
were fine animals and in no time at all a farmer from
Carlow bought them and gave James a good price. As was
the custom, the buyer and the seller went to a bar to drink
a luck-penny cup. Mary joined them and the farmer's wife
who was already waiting in the bar after her morning's
shopping. When Mary entered, she stared quizzically at
her. After a drink or two, the Carlow man told James that
his bride was 'the spit' of his own daughter, whom he had
buried many years before. The farmer's wife added, 'I
thought the same as soon as I clapped eyes on her.' James
asked them the date of their daughter's death. It coincided
with the day he had seen the girl step from the coffin. The
old farmer's wife stared at Mary again and said, 'Pull down
the top of your dress, allanah.' Mary's retort stunned the
other three. She said, 'It's all right, mother. The raspberry
mark is still on my shoulder.'

Those who regarded Moll Anthony as being in league
with the good people said she was that girl, Mary (Moll).
But this type of story rightly upsets some logical thinkers.
Some of them claim that Moll Anthony's father was an

Anthony Dunne and that she got her name from him, because if a few families of the same name lived in an area, it was normal to append the father's Christian name to distinguish his daughter.

But what about the mysterious Milltown tombstones?

Well, Lord Walter Fitzgerald claimed that Moll Anthony's name was Leeson, that she died in 1878 and that her cure passed on to another James Leeson. This man lived in 'a comfortable slated house on the Hill of Grange' on the site of Moll's former mud-walled house. Local people accept that James had the cure and that the house that still clings to the side of Grange Hill was indeed his.

Through the ivy on one of the Milltown stones can be read the inscription:

Erected by Catherine Leeson of Grange Hill in memory of her dearly beloved husband, James Leeson, who departed this life 27 [or 22?] April 1894. Aged 64 years.

The legend on the bare stone beside it is difficult to read but it seems to be:

Erected by Mary Leeson of Punchesgrange in memory of her mother, Eliza Cronley [or Cronboy?] who departed this life 11 of Dec. 1851, aged 20 years. Also the above named Mary Leeson who died 28 Nov. 1878, aged 71 years.

Now Mary Leeson, born in 1807, could not have had a mother who died in 1851, aged 20. Eliza Cronley could possibly have been her mother if she died in 1851, aged 90, and a close study reveals that somebody could have tampered with the 9 to make a 2 in Eliza Cronley's age at death.

Was this a deliberate attempt to make the inscription appear ridiculous?

Was Sir Walter Fitzgerald right when he said that Moll Anthony's father was Anthony Dunne? Was it propriety that deterred him from mentioning an unmarried mother, because a child born out of wedlock at the turn of the nineteenth century got little in the way of kindness — not even her own name when grown up and decently married?

The evidence available seems to present conclusive proof that Mary Leeson was the lady known as Moll Anthony. Kildare folklore links her curing powers with the fairy folk who lived in the heart of the Hill of Allen. This was the headquarters of the ancient Fianna; it was also the place first visited by Oisín on his return from Tír na n-Óg. The Hill of Allen, the Red Hills, the bleak Hill of Grange — old people tell strange tales of the supernatural by firesides in and around all three areas, and in most of them, Moll Anthony figures, a mortal among, if not definitely of, the *sidhe*.

SIX

Fionn Mac Cumhaill and the Sidhe

No collection of Irish fairy tales would be complete without recalling one of the many brushes between the legendary chieftain, Fionn Mac Cumhaill, and the *sidhe*. Fionn led the Fianna, a band of warriors who acted as bodyguards to the High Kings of Ireland. Their fortress headquarters was at the Hill of Allen in County Kildare. He was far away from there one day, hunting with his hounds, Bran and Sceólan, and some of his band. They came to a hill in Breffni, which was in the Cavan region, and as they hunted, the king of the Breffni *sidhe*, Conaran, watched them from his earthen keep, Dún Conaran. Conaran envied Fionn his power and his army. At one stage in the hunt, Fionn, his hounds and his colleague Conn became separated from the rest of the Fianna. Conaran saw this as a chance to destroy Fionn.

The fairy king had three daughters. They were the ugliest and worst-tempered girls in the fairy kingdom. Their eyes were like bloodshot onions, and their noses as crooked as rams' horns. Donkeys' ears would have been prettier than theirs. Hair grew outside and inside lips that drooped to their breasts, revealing stumps of black teeth that were the shape of tombstones. It must have slipped down from their heads, because these were thatched with leeches and filthy brown reeds. When they spoke, they sounded like boars at mating time. The dreadful laughing of the Crooked Crones from Cork would have sounded like sweet music if compared with the tittering of this trio, Cuillean, Caébhóg and Iarainn. They seldom laughed, of course, and when they did, it was either at someone else's plight or to harm a human. The laugh of the *sidhe* can do untold harm.

Conaran called these daughters to look at Fionn and each one of them cackled and writhed with longing, because women of the *sidhe* are fond of human warriors. They drew their nails, that were like ravens' talons, through their leeches and studied themselves in a stream to make sure they looked all right. When they were inside the fort, you see, these girls did not realise they were ugly. And another thing, human eyes saw them as beautiful beings.

The women sat a few feet inside the entrance to the fairy fort and began spinning. Each had yarn wound around a hazel branch so that it would weave a spell. Fionn and Conn came by and noticed them. In order to get a better look, they stepped inside the boundary between their world and that of the *sidhe*. Even before they pushed the hazels aside, they were under a spell, but when they touched the wood of the branch, each of their hands felt as heavy as the Rock of Dunamase and a withering weakness trembled in their bodies. This made their necks flop about like eels, while their legs wobbled and finally collapsed beneath them.

'Your whiskers are the most beautiful things I ever saw,' Fionn said to Caébhóg. The fairy wench smiled and, luckily, Fionn closed his eyes to think, because he still realised that they were in some danger and wanted to devise some way of calling the rest of the Fianna to his assistance. If his eyes had been open, the smile would have pierced his heart.

Conn looked at Iarainn and said, 'I have travelled the length and breadth of Ireland and paid a visit or two to

Alba also, but never have I seen eyes and ears as delightful as yours.' Iarainn blushed and the redness would have blinded Conn, but he too closed his eyes, the more to dwell on the apparent pulchritude of Iarainn. Before he opened them, he heard Fionn say, 'Whistle up the Fianna, Conn.' Conn vaguely remembered how he was renowned for sounding a note that carried across the western world. He smiled as he remembered how a lark from Greece once came to the Hill of Allen in answer to his whistle. So he pursed his lips to call the Fianna, but no sound came, only a kind of 'phut phut' that you would hear when porridge was beginning to boil. He wept, and Iarainn licked the tears from his face. Conn thought this was the gentlest touch he had ever experienced. Fionn looked at him, however, and was horrified at what he saw. Conn's face was bleeding, because the coarse hairs on Iarainn's tongue were like briars. The three harridans then tied up the two men with ropes of plaited bracken and danced around them gleefully. Cuillean went to her father and hugged him and asked him to allow herself and her sisters to do something terrible to Fionn and Conn. An evil grin spread across Conaran's face, but he told his daughter to have patience, because there were more of the Fianna to come. Fionn Mac Cumhaill heard this. His mighty intellect sensed further danger and he began to resist the fairy spell. He opened one eye slightly and noticed that the three women were not quite as beautiful as they had first appeared. He closed it quickly in order to concentrate more.

Meanwhile, Bran and Sceólan were barking at the entrance to the fairy fort. Animals can always detect the supernatural, so their baying became louder and louder

when their master did not reappear. The remainder of
the Fianna huntsmen were chasing a magnificent black
hog towards the Leitrim border, but they heard the
barking, called off the chase and returned to Dún
Conaran. There they saw the anxiety of Bran and
Sceólan at the entrance to the fairy fort. Realising that
their leader was in some danger, they rushed in,
sweeping the hazel branches aside. Immediately, they
suffered the same debility as Fionn and Conn. The three
women tied them all up and Cuillean winked at her
father and said she knew what he had meant earlier.
They trussed some of the men as fowl waiting for
roasting and rolled them into a dark cave, all the time
screaming with glee. Others, they laid side by side and
leaped up and down on their stomachs. They stood
Conn on his head in a damp hole and allowed slugs and
snails to crawl into his mouth, his nose and ears.
Cuillean brought Fionn into a small, private cave and
kissed him until his mouth festered.

When it was time to close up the fort for the night,
Conaran told Caébhóg to go outside and see if she could
do anything about the dogs' baying.

'We won't sleep a wink tonight after the fun,' he said,
leering. As he said this, he honed his sword and Caébhóg
shivered with excitement.

'Don't start any slaying until I return,' she demanded,
with delight.

Caébhóg went outside. A bright moon slid from
behind a rugged black cloud and she began to raise her
arms to cast a dog-silencing spell on the animals. At that
moment a lame man hobbled towards the fort. It was the
great fighter of the Fianna, Goll Mac Morna, who had
twisted his ankle and had dropped behind the others when

they responded to the call of the hounds. A former leader
of the Fianna, Goll was celebrated among the fairy folk
as a formidable opponent. Therefore, Caébhóg decided to
kill him before he entered the fort. She called in to her
sisters and they came to her side. All three drew their
swords and faced Goll.

'Each one of us is worth a hundred of the Fianna,'
they threatened, as they called on Goll to do battle.

Goll too drew his sword and, although his ankle
gave him great pain, he leaped forty feet into the air,
letting out a war-cry that was heard in Wales. A man
from Pembrokeshire thought it was the archangel's
trumpet announcing the end of the world. Goll's foot
hurt when he landed, but so did Caébhóg's head, because
his heel hit her crown and drove her three feet into the
boggy earth.

As always happens when the *sidhe* do battle with
humans, the earth stood still, and everything on it became
silent. The winds stopped blowing, the clouds ceased to
move and the moon turned red. Some hounds were
caught standing on their hind legs. Others balanced on
three paws. Bran and Sceólan lay head to head, feet in
the air. There was no more barking.

Only the combatants moved, and the swishing of
their weapons made an eerie noise, the only sound heard
for the next three hours of that night. Time and time
again, the women lunged at Conn but always he dodged
them and slashed some part of their bodies with his
sword. No matter how deeply he gashed them, there was
just a small spurt of yellow blood before the wound
healed. As time passed, however, his foot became swollen.
It looked like a huge turnip and was the same hue. The
weight of this lump made Goll tire terribly, and his

battle-leaps barely brought him above the trees. He realised that he must end the fight or be slain.

Goll dropped his sword to his side. Thinking he was too tired to keep it aloft, the three women screamed with delight and formed a semicircle as they moved towards him to deliver their death thrust. When they were within six feet of him, Goll swung his sword in a mighty arc and sliced the trio in two. Three upper bodies still lashed out with swords, while three lower bodies ran around Conn, trying to trip him up. He approached the upper halves first and split each one from head to navel so that only the sword arm remained a threat. Then he kicked at the lower halves with his good foot. One of these landed in Donegal, another in Mayo and a third in west Kerry. Only the first landed on hard ground and today it is called Errigal Mountain. The others sank in marshland, and that is why people in Mayo and Kerry call this type of ground 'bottoms'.

Goll sliced off the wrist of each sword-hand then. As soon as he did, the earth trembled, the winds blew and the moon regained its former colour. The hounds leaped about and ate the bits of woman that remained scattered around. Inside Dún Conaran, the bindings fell away from Fionn and the Fianna. When Conaran saw this, he made himself disappear while the warriors uttered a great roar and dashed from the fort to clasp Goll Mac Morna in grateful embrace.

Led by their hounds, the Fianna then faced south and headed for their Hill of Allen home. They were in good spirits, singing and shouting. They were not gone a mile, however, when they heard a piercing wail and, looking behind them, they beheld a fearsome sight.

Now when Conaran the fairy king was married first,
his queen lost a daughter in childbirth because she was
delivered outside the fairy fort. Before they buried the
infant under a thorn tree, they named her Brón, which
means sorrow. It is fairy practice that an infant so
deceased can re-emerge fully grown, should any human
take the life of one of its siblings. Since Goll had killed
three sisters, therefore, Brón returned three times the
size of each sister, three times as ugly and uttering threats
in a voice that was louder and more grating than
anything the Fianna had ever heard before. This freak
had no hair at all, but a scalp of granite. Her eyes
protruded like two sheeps' bladders and her nose was
the shape of the Sugarloaf mountain in Wicklow, and
not much smaller. From ears that looked like sides of
beef, plants that resembled enormous nettles grew.
The woman was at least twenty feet tall. Not being
inside the fairy fort, her grotesqueness was evident to
the Fianna.

'I demand revenge for the slaying of my sisters,' she
roared, and six large oak trees fell before the thunder of
her voice.

'To this you have a right,' said Fionn, calling on his
son Oisín to oblige. To everybody's horror, for the likes of
this never happened before, Oisín refused, saying he had
lost the power of his arms. Scornfully, Fionn called on his
grandson Oscar, but he too declined for a similar reason.
One after another, men who were famous for their
bravery refused to fight this ogress. Eventually, Goll Mac
Morna spoke.

'It was I who killed this woman's sisters, so let me
attempt to do battle with her.' By this time the lump on
his ankle was as big as Mount Leinster and Fionn was

reluctant to allow him to face such a formidable foe. Goll
insisted and the fight began. The noise of battle rang
throughout the land making a din that was surpassed only
by Brón's terrifying shouts. Goll knew he had to win
quickly, because his strength was ebbing. As in the fight
with Cuillean, Caébhóg and Iarainn, he dropped his
sword-arm and Brón thought he was unable to continue.
She lunged forward, Goll side-stepped and slashed off her
right leg. She toppled and fell against a giant oak, which
collapsed under her weight. As it fell, a large branch struck
her and stunned her. Goll Mac Morna moved in and cut
off her head with his sword. As he held it in the air, the
Fianna cheered him. Fionn complimented him and told
him he would reward him with his most cherished
possession.

'I have a beautiful daughter called Cebha,' he said
to Goll.

'You have indeed,' said Goll.

'You may take her in marriage,' Fionn promised.

Goll thanked him. The couple married and lived
happily for a while. Like many who achieve greatness,
however, Goll brooded on how he saved Fionn and the
Fianna and on how his own father had lost the leadership
to Fionn. This injustice, as he saw it, preyed on him until
he became sullen and bad-tempered. He did not know
this, but the *sidhe* were putting all sorts of evil notions
into his head. They arranged a quarrel between Goll
and Fionn's son Cairell, getting Cairell to say 'You keep
boasting about your great feat. My father would have
killed Cuillean, Caébhóg and Iarainn himself but for
the fact that, within the fairy fort, they looked beautifully
feminine and it would have broken the rules of the
Fianna to harm them.'

'Your father was afraid of them,' accused Goll.
They fought and Goll cut off his brother-in-law's head.
An angry Fionn Mac Cumhaill came across his dead son.
Letting out a great wail of grief, he drew his sword and
slew Goll Mac Morna.

Ever after, before every hunt, he warned the Fianna
not to go near a fairy fort.

SEVEN

Biddy Mannion's Baby

On Inishark, off the Connemara coast, a woman called
Biddy Mannion gave birth to a baby. At an early age
the boy child was the spit of his handsome father and
some said he was the fairest fellow ever born to a
fisherman's wife. Biddy breast-fed her infant. This, the
neighbours said, was beneficial to the child's health. At the
same time, the king and queen of the sea fairies had a son,
but the queen, God help her, was not too good at the
nursing. It was not entirely her fault, because she was
pining for her blackguard of a husband. Right through her
confinement and after, this reprobate was away up around
the Giant's Causeway having some sort of argument with
another royal fairy who had come across from Scotland to
cause trouble. As a result, the Scottish fairy had cursed the
queen's lactation. The distraught queen employed a wet-
nurse, a female seal that lived in a cave on the mainland
near Cleggan. The plan was not successful. Seals are
enchanted members of the Kanes who in the distant past
were not too successful at breast-feeding either.

Biddy Mannion, therefore, was under observation by
the special branch of the *sidhe*. She had a protection
racket going for her, however. A *bean feasa* (wise woman)
gave her some charms to ward off the wee folk. These
included a charred turf-sod from a Saint John's Night
bonfire, which she placed under the baby's mattress. One
night the child cried and Biddy took him into her own
bed to feed. The little lad soon satisfied himself and fell
asleep. Biddy left him in her own bed while she went to
the kitchen for a cup of tea. While there, three dark men

entered, took her outside, threw her across one of their
horses and galloped away. There were only a few splashes
as the steeds crossed the water and sped along the coast.
They came to a splendid house that Biddy had never
seen before. Indeed, she had never heard of anything
more than a thatched cabin or two near Cleggan. A
young gentleman dressed in gold and silver garments
greeted her and led her indoors. He brought Biddy to a
room where a young woman sat knitting. When she
looked up, this stranger had a concerned expression on
her face. Biddy asked why she was staring at her and the
lady replied that she was recalling her own first night in
the house. She had eaten and drunk to her heart's
content, an unwise thing to do. It was magic fare and, by
partaking of it, she became a prisoner. She advised Biddy
to abstain. 'And when you get home, please ask my
husband, Tim Conneely, to use his influence with the
Abbot of Cong to get me reinstated on the national
census,' she begged.

There was a knock on the door and her host opened
it. Mrs Conneely disappeared but another worried-
looking woman stood in her place. She held a baby. The
young gentlemen took this and gave it to Biddy, asking
her to suckle it. She did.

Afterwards, they led Biddy to a huge dining room.
The tables were laden with the best of food and drink.
Lords and ladies sat in sartorial splendour but they did not
sneer at Biddy's worn and faded raiment. The queen of
the *sidhe* sat at the top table and beckoned Biddy to take
the seat beside her. Poor Biddy was ravenous after her
journey, but she remembered Mrs Conneely's warning and
refused the queen's hospitality. Instead, she requested a
cure for a sick child belonging to a neighbour on Inishark.

'Take ten green rushes from beside a well at Aughavalla,' the queen instructed. 'Throw away the tenth one and squeeze the sap of the other nine into a taycup. Give this potion to the child to drink.'

Biddy was surprised at the queen's pronunciation, because her accent was otherwise quite cultured. Indeed, Biddy later described the queen as being 'like an English woman'.

Just then, the king of the fairies arrived back from his shenanigans. The queen told him what had happened and he gave Biddy a gold ring in appreciation. 'It will keep you from hurt and harm,' he promised. Then he rubbed ointment on her eyes and immediately she found herself in a dark, damp cave. A female seal saw her and rushed out squealing. There was a musty smell and, looking around, Biddy saw hundreds of human skeletons. The fairy king was by her side and he explained.

'These are not as they seem to you. They are the fallen angels that you mortals call fairies.' He led her to another chamber. All around it, young blindfolded children sat still upon toadstools. They did not speak and the stillness was eerie. The king whispered, 'The souls of children who died without baptism.'

'Am I in limbo, then?' Biddy asked, but received no answer. Instead, the king led her out of the cave where the sea waves rose and fell, yet were not made of water, but of grass and flowers. They walked through these. They gradually faded and withered until Biddy realised that she was back at the lane that led to her own cottage on Inishark.

'See who comes to greet you!' the fairy king exclaimed.

When Biddy looked, her escort disappeared. Who was coming down the boreen but her double. The two Biddy

Mannions met and became one. Biddy raced into the
house to discover her child sleeping peacefully where
she had left him. Her husband came back from fishing,
looked at her and shouted, 'Who the blazes gave you that
expensive ring?'

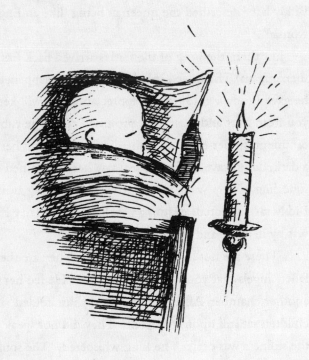

EIGHT

The House on the Rath

Much has been written about fairy raths and fairy paths, places where the wee folk frisk and play or have right of way. The gable wall of a Leitrim church was built on a fairy rath and the whole edifice jumped into the next field. Ill-luck befell many families who dared build on a *slígh sidhe* (fairy pass), Jim Johnson, for instance, a man from the North who settled in the West and was one sandwich short of a picnic. This was evident when he refused the warnings of neighbours about a proposed building site. They had seen the fairy host, the *slua sidhe*, dancing on a rath near Knockcroghery and would not walk across it, let alone build on it. It was there that Johnson erected a mansion of fine Wicklow granite and Cavan slate. Its interior was of carved oak and elm and a finer house was never seen west of the Boyne. Their only child, a lively 10-year-old boy wanted for nothing. He had magnificent hand-carved toys, a small pony, a donkey and a pet hen. Mrs Johnson wore gold-trimmed gowns, elegant hats and shoes, even when attending to her housekeeping. People quipped that Jim Johnson must have found the fairies' own gold in the foundations, so ostentatious was the building. Just as fine were the gardens that he set around it, all full of flowers and fruit and vegetables. The Johnsons had everything they desired, except visitors, because no neighbour would enter a house built on a fairy rath.

Jim Johnson held a house warming but nobody came to it. He, his wife and son were eating the unused food for a week and there was still plenty left when an old

woman came to the door looking for a billy-can full of
milk. Mrs Johnson refused. The old lady took off her blue
cloak and waved it overhead as she said, 'I am asking a
second and last time. Give me some milk from your fine
herd, said to give the best yield in the land.' Again Mrs
Johnson refused. Indeed, she called her servants and told
them to chase the woman off the estate.

Next day, Jim Johnson went to the byre. His finest
milch cow lay moaning and dribbling. He sent servants for
a wise woman who lived in the neighbourhood and had
plenty of healing mixtures. She would not come. Two days
later, Mrs Johnson ordered her kitchen staff to bake bread.
She left the kitchen and was knitting in the garden when
the little woman in the blue cloak scurried out from
behind a gooseberry bush.

'Your maids are working at the griddles,' she said.
'Please give me some fresh cake.'

'You killed our best cow. Be off with yourself,' Mrs
Johnson scolded.

Again the old woman begged and again the mistress
had her servant chase her away.

Over the next few days, young Johnson lost all his
lively ways. He fretted about the house and turned pallid
and listless. One morning he told his mother that the
fairies stopped him from sleeping, that they jumped up
and down on his chest until he could hardly breathe.
'They keep asking me for a billy-can of milk and a griddle
cake', he said. So Mrs Johnson gave him these things to
bring to his room that night. Next morning they were
gone and the boy said that he had got a great night's sleep.
His feeling of well-being soon left him, however, and he
continued to fail. His eyes became dull and his limbs weak
and when his parents asked him if he could explain it, he

said, 'I am exhausted from dancing with the *sidhe*. Each
night they take me through the floor, deep below the
rath on which the house stands. There I dance with the
loveliest of ladies, I eat the finest food and drink the finest
wine, but I never feel well. Please save me, mother and
father. Get a priest to bless me or they will take me away
altogether.'

Scorning both religion and the fairies, the Johnsons
were dubious, but to please their son they sent for a priest.
As soon as the holy man prayed over the boy, he took on
a pleasant countenance and seemed tranquil within
himself. He fell into a deep sleep. Next morning his
parents were full of hope when he told them that he had
not been dancing with the fairies. They were delighted,

but their joy changed to sorrow when he continued,
'Last night I dwelt with the angels. I roamed through a
beautiful garden where everything was calm and peaceful.
The angels told me that I would be back for good by
nightfall.' And he was. Before midnight he told his mother
that the angels were coming for him, and as the village
clock struck the hour, he passed away peacefully, a sweet
smile playing around his lips.

Jim Johnson was shattered. He neglected his farm and
took to drinking heavily. His crops went unattended, his
cattle remained unmilked and died bellowing. On the
anniversary of his son's death, he too passed away. Full of
fear, neighbours ignored Mrs Johnson, so she packed her
belongings and went home to her own people in Sligo.

Lawyers put the Johnson property on the market to
clear debts. A Knockcroghery man bought it, but the first
thing he did after the acquisition was to pull down the
house built on the rath. The land then produced the best
crops in all Connaught; the cattle produced the biggest
yield ever known since the legendary white cow, Bó Fin,
came out of the western sea to help make Ireland a land of
milk and honey; the grass grew again on the rath; and the
lively music of the sidhe was heard from it every night of a
full moon and during all the major festivals.

No woman in the vicinity ever wore a cloak of blue
until ten years and a day after the demolition of the
Johnson mansion.

NINE

Madge Moran of Meath

M.J. Molloy's play, *Petticoat Loose*, featured a fearsome fairy woman who indulged in all sorts of demonic rites. It reminded playgoers that at one time every district, barony or parish in Ireland had its own 'wise man', 'knowing woman', or 'fairy person' (the *sidhe* were early into these terms of the liberated!). According to local beliefs, these people 'had the gift', that is, they could counsel, cure or kill — well, almost. Country people feared some, dreaded a few, shunned others, but sought after most of them.

Westmeath had Conor Sheridan, the fairy doctor of Lough Bawn; Rathangan, County Kildare, had Moll Anthony; and Royal Meath had Madge Moran of Balrath.

An old woman, with hair turned back on all sides, Madge was very tiny and very neat. She dressed in a red cloak and a crisp white cap. Yet, she had an evil countenance. Her wrinkled face tapered into a pinched, pointed chin and harassed mothers threatened her on many a bold child. Madge lived in a 'bottoms', a swampy marsh near a small lake close to where Saint Scire, the great-great grandniece of Niall of the Nine Hostages, established a nunnery. Madge's most famous case concerned Terence McGrath, only son of a respectable farmer, and Alice Moore, the daughter of a small farmer. In those days 'respectable' suggested wealth rather than propriety.

Terence was a spoiled lad. His parents doted over him and gave him everything but a good trouncing that would have done him all the good in the world. He grew up a handsome man-about-Balrath, and was fond of wine,

women and himself. Alas, poor young Alice Moore fell
in love with him, and soon the pair were contemplating
marriage. His parents did not approve of Terence's
intentions and his father exhorted him to 'look a bit
higher and have some of the McGrath spirit'. Perhaps
Terence misunderstood his father's advice, but in any case
after a few secret meetings with Alice the poor girl
became pregnant. The rogue kept away then all right and
his delighted parents covered up for him. They spread a
rumour that their son was about to marry a 'girl of his
own station' whose father had more than a few acres of
prime fattening land on Boyneside.

Meanwhile the distracted Alice went to consult
Madge Moran who seemed to relish the assignment,
remarking, 'McGrath was always a jackeen since a yard
made him a coat.' She had disliked the youth since the day
he accused her of having truck with the good people.
Poor Alice had only a half a crown to offer Madge and the
old woman scraped at her pipe a while before consenting
to help. 'I'll do it but don't ever tell the mother that bore
you or the priest that christened you.' Then she told Alice
to come the following night and to bring three flannel
sheets, three candles, a sheaf of clean corn and some
refreshments. They would need the refreshments because
they would be working all night, Madge explained. When
questioned about the work, she shrieked in delight and
described how, from the stroke of midnight, they would
be digging a grave for a young man.

A bright young girl was Alice. She immediately saw
the sinister implications and refused to be a party to them.
She offered to wait until she could raise some extra money
for a less drastic remedy. Madge agreed. Alice worked hard
to earn the cash and then she had another consultation.

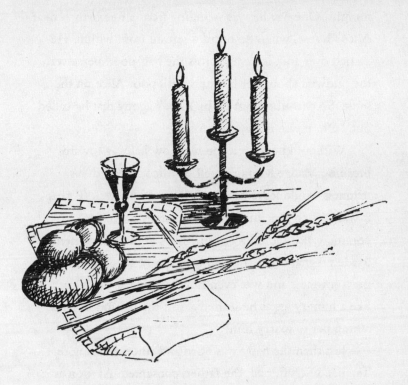

This time, Madge prescribed a powder that she had in an old snuff-box. She ordered Alice to send for Terence and to put it in his tea. Alice, proud girl, refused to invite the scoundrel to tea, so Madge administered the powder herself and the fellow went stark raving mad. He roared and screamed, sped wildly through the woods, tearing his flesh with briars, catching young rabbits and eating them raw. Farmers tied down their haycocks because he had a habit of kicking them out of his way. Schoolchildren ran home when they saw him, because one day he caught a little boy by the arm and flung him into the middle of the next parish.

Horrified, Mr and Mrs McGrath engaged all sorts of doctors and specialists. Each and every one of them was perplexed, and Terence remained a maniac for four

months. One day he was swinging from a tree branch near
Alice's house, when he heard a scream from within. He
dashed over and, looking across the half-door, perceived
the midwife about her business with poor Alice on the
settle. So perturbed was he by Alice's agony that he called
out, 'Oh, please marry me, Alice.'

Without knowing it, he was now halfway towards
breaking Madge Moran's spell. If Alice accepted, his
madness would leave him and all would be well. (Perhaps
it was at such junctures that fairy serials broke for
commercials!) Could a girl in Alice's condition consent?
Made pregnant by a man who ran away, who developed a
great madness and was even now frothing at the mouth
like a hungry ass as he leaned across the half-door! And
asking her to marry him!

Just then the baby was born and Alice, realising that
Terence was, after all, the father, consented. As soon as
she did, Terence became his old self again. More — he
developed a bit of backbone and went up to his parents,
boldly proclaiming that he was about to marry Alice.

This he did. Some people even say that Madge Moran
was matron-of-honour at the wedding!

TEN

The Rathcoffey Pooka

F airy lore in some parts of Ireland projected the pooka as a phantom goat that contaminated wells and crops. In most areas it was a giant black horse that often galloped on cloven hooves like the devil. Within the fine mansion of Hamilton Rowan in Rathcoffey, County Kildare, however, the pooka appeared as a big donkey.

It was during the Rising of 1798 and the great landowner was abroad. The servants still cooked for themselves and for the farm hands, so there was always plenty of crockery for washing up after meals. In the master's absence, when the last meal of the day was over, the household left the dirty dishes in the scullery until the following morning. They sat around the fire in the huge kitchen and amused themselves telling ghost stories. This was mock bravery, because nobody ever referred to something that caused great worry each night: the banging and clattering of kitchen utensils, pokers, tongs and bellows, all accompanied by loud laughter. There was a good side to it, because each morning the delf stood gleaming on the shelves, the fire was blazing merrily in the hearth and the kitchen and scullery were spotless. Each servant hoped some of the others had risen early to tidy up, but was afraid to enquire. There could have been a more sinister explanation.

One night, the story-telling took longer than usual. A scullery boy could not get near the fire, and he did not understand some of the yarns being spun. Somewhat bored, he crept under the settle bed, covered himself with a rug and fell asleep. Nobody noticed this, and when the

last servant raked the fire with ashes, put out the lamp and
went to bed, the lad continued sleeping. Awakened by the
sound of the back door opening, he pulled down the rug
and peeped out. A big donkey was closing the door with
a flick of his tail. The boy rubbed his eyes to make sure he
was not dreaming, but the animal sauntered over to the
fire and sat on his haunches. It looked into the ashes for a
while, then yawned and spoke in a peculiar bray. 'I
suppose I might as well begin.'

The terrified boy thought the donkey was going to
begin eating him, but instead, it took the poker and stirred
up the fire. Then it placed some turf on it and settled a
cauldron on the hook. It fetched the water bucket, which
was empty. 'Humph!' it grunted, then went to the well
and filled it. While it was away, the boy got himself into a
corner where he could see more without being discovered.

The donkey returned, filled the cauldron and sat
with its back to the boy, waiting for it to boil. The animal
began to sing but stopped suddenly after one verse and
shouted, 'I suppose you think I can't see you, young
fellow.' With that, it swung around and grabbed the boy.
It held him over the cauldron and the wee fellow
screamed with fear. Then the pooka flung him back in
under the settle where the poor lad's teeth chattered
with fright. It kept guffawing and, in a dance-like motion,
went about the kitchen dusting shelves, washing the table
and sweeping the floor. The water in the cauldron
bubbled, so the pooka took it to the scullery and the
boy heard it laughing more as it washed and dried all
the crockery and put each item in its proper place. The
lad wondered how an ass could know so much. When
everything was tidy, the pooka raked the fire again and
took one last look around. 'They will think you a great
scullery lad,' it brayed, and laughed its way out into
the night.

Next morning, the boy told his story. Some of the
maids believed him; others did not. A clever lass from
Staplestown suggested that they should do no more
washing or ironing or cleaning, but leave everything for
the pooka to look after. All agreed, and all day they had
a great time lazing about and telling stories.

That night, the scullery boy made sure to be in bed
early. The other servants stayed a while chatting, but
before midnight all retired for the night and slept. Next
morning, each one approached the kitchen full of
anticipation. The plan had worked: the housework had
been attended to and everything was spotless.

As time passed by, the household got lazier and lazier.
Some servants took to drinking and the farm hands

complained that, while the kitchen was spotless, the
staff were neglecting their cooking duties. They heard the
stories about the pooka and wished they could persuade it
to take on outdoor chores. With this in mind, a
ploughman sneaked into the kitchen one night when the
servants had gone to bed. The pooka arrived and the
ploughman spoke up.

'You are making the servants here lazy, sir. Why do
you not come in daylight for a change and maybe do a bit
of ploughing or harrowing or pulping mangolds?'

'My good man,' said the pooka, 'I must do all my
work in the kitchen and scullery.'

'And why, pray?' the ploughman asked.

'Sit down there and I'll tell you,' said the ass.

They sat. The ploughman offered the pooka a drag of
his pipe and thought he noticed the animal flinch as it
refused. It began nervously.

'When Master Hamilton Rowan was an infant, I was
a servant here. Although a lazy human, I received kind
treatment from your master's father. He gave me shelter,
clothing, food, even a few drinks, but I was the world's
worst idler. A sick sparrow would do more in a week than
I did in my lifetime. So, when I died and faced the Eternal
Judge, he chastised me and said that before saving my
immortal soul, I would have to become an enchanted
animal attending to the *sidhe*, a pooka. To add to my
shame, I would appear in the form of that most derided
beast, the donkey. I would take on all the chores that I had
neglected while alive. I would have to be cheerful about it
too. This completed, I would have to go back out into the
night and stand frozen in a wet fairy rath until morning,
when the wee folk would find something else for me to
do. So you see, my good man, I cannot perform your tasks

for you, but must slave away here each night and laugh at my own misery.'

The ploughman was sorry for himself, because he could not get the pooka to perform his duties. But he was sorry for the animal too. So too was one of the servants. On being awakened by the commotion, she had crept downstairs and overheard the conversation. She came into the kitchen, carrying her best red wool coat. 'You have been very good to us, sir,' she said. 'Take this coat and keep yourself warm.'

The girl and the ploughman helped the animal into the coat. They stuck the two forelegs in each arm and buttoned the garment across the creature as if it were human.

'Give me a mirror until I see myself,' said the ass. They did this and the pooka laughed louder than ever and thanked the donor profusely. With its dance-like steps, it waltzed around the kitchen floor, then lifted the latch and slid out into the night.

'Wait! Wait!' shouted the servant. 'What about the washing and cleaning? You haven't attended to that!'

'And I won't any more,' brayed the pooka, 'because now I am free. My punishment was to last until somebody appreciated my labours enough to give me a reward. You have done this and I thank you. But now I am released from my obligation, from the fairies and from my pledge. My soul is saved and I will depart this earth for ever.' So saying, the pooka galloped into the night. As it passed the Green Hill near Donadea, it let a last long laugh and a wise woman who lived there stirred in her bed, nudged her husband and said, 'He who laughs best laughs last.'

From that day to this, nobody ever showed proper appreciation of the great things achieved by Kildare men.

ELEVEN

The Churchyard Bride

The Leannán Sidhe was a fairy lover, normally female, who inspired poets in return for their love. Occasionally it was male and sometimes it could adopt either form. When such was the case, it struck particular terror into the hearts of country people, because a bisexual fairy could be the Devil himself.

A tiny churchyard in Erigle Truagh, in the barony of Truagh, County Monaghan, was unique in that it had its own Leannán Sidhe. This fairy watched over corpses buried in the stony earth, but often left its post to tempt poetic relatives of the dead. At funerals it took particular note of the person who was last to leave the graveside, normally the person who composed the epitaph of the deceased. That person was almost certainly paid a visit during the following weeks — if something more dreadful did not occur.

You see, the Leannán Sidhe could actually approach the mourner on the spot. If it was a male, the Leannán Sidhe took on the form of a beautiful young woman who inspired the swain with a charmed passion, kissed him and promised to meet him a month from that day, when he would compose brilliant verse.

The trouble was, however, that as soon as the young besotted fellow left the churchyard, he remembered the local tradition and became deeply depressed, because tradition declared that the man so kissed would be buried in the same cemetery on the same day of the following month. Similarly, if the tarrying mourner was a poetess, a fairy in male form seduced her.

One such victim had just been married and was madly loved by her handsome young husband. He composed a song called 'The Churchyard Bride' after the lovely young Aileen O'More fell victim to the Spectre of Death, the Fairy of Erigle Truagh, the Leannán Sidhe. Fittingly, the sad story is recorded in verse, often sung to the air of 'The Dawning of the Day'.

The night was calm, and a clear full moon
Was beaming o'er hill and lea,
As I parted my true-love all too soon,
Beneath the trysting tree.
My thoughts flowed on to the morrow's noon —
To the hour so long deferred;
When away down the vale rose a doleful wail,
And this is what I heard:
Aileen O'More! Aileen asthore!
From thine earthly bondage come;
Aileen O'More! on the fairy shore
Thy kindred call thee home.

I hastened back to the myrtle bower,
I found my darling there,
Her form bent low like a faded flower,
The death dew on her hair.
I clasped her hand — Ah, why did I cower!
No pulse within it stirred.
Whilst once again that dolorous strain
In the haunted vale I heard:
Aileen O'More! Aileen asthore!
From thine earthly bondage come;
Aileen O'More! on the fairy shore
Thy kindred call thee home.

In a lonely nook we laid her at rest,
And we decked her grave with flowers;
But their bloom was crushed by my heaving breast
Through all the weary hours —
Till the midnight came, when a phantom guest
Stood nigh where my love was interred;
As she stole away in the dawn of day
This warning voice I heard:
Phelim, asthore! Weep no more,
For soon the time will come,
When, thy bondage o'er to the spirit-shore,
Thy bride will bear thee home!

TWELVE

The Magic Lapwing

The lapwing, known in Ireland as the *pilibín*, is white
with black and green upper parts. It is also called a
pee-wit, after its excited call that rises on the second
syllable. An Pilibín Glas Bán (the Green-white Lapwing)
was one such specimen. This bird conveyed messages from
the fairies of the West of Ireland to certain mortals. It was
particularly attentive to people of royal blood.

Once upon a time, an eagle led the birds of the air in
a fight against the rodents of Clare. A prince supported the
animals. The birds won and the prince, in a fit of rage,
fired his gun and wounded the eagle. He brought the bird
home and locked it in a royal stable for a year and a day,
giving it nothing but water and an occasional fistful of
oats. When he finally released the bird, it flew away,
shouting as it did: 'You treated me badly for a year and a
day. I now curse you to a life of wandering. You will never
sleep two nights in the same bed or eat two meals at the
same table until you find An Pilibín Glas Bán.'

The prince was due to marry the lovely daughter of a
wealthy merchant, so he asked his father's advice. The king
said he had no option but to obey An Pilibín Glas Bán.
He then gave his son two cakes of soda bread, his best
steed and sent him away in search of the fairy bird.

The prince rode well and covered many miles before
darkness fell. He tethered his horse and lay down under a
large oak tree, covering himself with moss and twigs.
Before he could get to sleep, a small weedy man came
along and called, 'Welcome to the son of the King of
Ireland!' The prince thanked him for his welcome but

asked how the man knew who he was. He replied,
'Never mind how I know your name or what you seek.
I cannot tell you the whereabouts of An Pilibín Glas Bán
tonight, but keep riding and tomorrow night I may have
some information.' This little man was a Fear Gurtha.
Such a fairy sometimes casts hungry grass (*fear gurtha*, not
to be confused with the thrower) beneath the feet of
travellers, causing them to waste away from hunger. At
other times, he tests the charity of mortals. This one was a
guide from the *sidhe*.

The Fear Gurtha was true to his word, and as the
prince began eating his first soda cake the next evening,
the little man appeared again and asked the prince for the
crumbs that fell on the earth. The prince offered him a
good thick slice of the bread and the Fear Gurtha ate it
ravenously. Then he told the prince that if he rode a little
more, he would pass the wood where An Pilibín Glas Bán
lived. The prince was pleased to learn that a beautiful
young woman would meet him.

'Her name is Sarah. When she looks at you, you
stare at her. When she laughs at you, you laugh at her.
When she tells you to come in with your horse, do so,'
the Fear Gurtha instructed. The prince did as he was told.
He met the girl, who beguiled him with her beauty. Her
hair was black and shiny like the ebony in the fireplace at
his father's palace. Large green eyes smiled from beneath
finely shaped brows and a strange misty aura enveloped
her face. Sarah invited him into the wood and led his
horse to a stable that stood beside a large purple house.
Then she told him that An Pilibín Glas Bán was awaiting
him inside.

Delighted at completing his quest so soon, the prince's
joy changed to shock when he entered. The small lapwing

revealed to him that he was the bird that he had kept
locked up and starving.

'But I shot at an eagle,' the prince protested.

'You shot me. I am the messenger of the *sidhe* and I
can take on many forms,' the *pilibín* lilted excitedly. 'And
I now command you to perform three tasks. If you fail, I
will behead you and send your head back to your father
on this.' An Pilibín Glas Bán seized a long sword from the
wall and brandished it wildly before disappearing.

Sarah returned then and led the prince to a bedroom
where he had a pleasant night's sleep. Next morning, she
prepared breakfast, but as soon as he dipped his spoon in
the egg, An Pilibín Glas Bán fluttered down from the
thatch and ordered him to work.

'Out you go to that hay shed, and we'll see how you
like a little ill-treatment, Prince. Take this grape [fork] and
move out all the straw, surely fifty tons of it, until you find
the needle my granny lost there last century. That should
settle your hash for you.'

The prince went to work, but for every forkful he
tossed out of the shed, two came back in. For every two
he threw out, four came in; for every four, eight; and so
on. Desperate, and fearing he would lose his life, the
prince worked until the perspiration ran from his body
and formed a stream outside the door. He cried too and
the stream became a torrent. From the swirling water
stepped Sarah, who told him that An Pilibín Glas Bán
would be out of the way for a while, reading a little and
having a short nap. 'Give me the fork,' she commanded.
The prince did do. She had the hay cleared in no time
and there, beneath, was the needle. She picked it up
and stuck it in the prince's lapel, telling him to give it to
An Pilibín Glas Bán.

When the bird came along later to inspect the work
and, no doubt, to have a good laugh at his former captor's
predicament, the prince gave him the needle. He became
greener with temper. 'Very good. You are the first man
ever to have completed the first task,' he said. Behind the
praise was the suspicion that his fairy daughter had worked
magic on the prince's behalf.

'Your second task will begin at dawn tomorrow. You
will plough and harrow the *bánóg*. It is small — only a
couple of acres — but it is my favourite green patch, so do
it well. Have a good sleep.' The prince detected a sneer on
his captor's bill. He rose and went to work at dawn. As
soon as he left the house, An Pilibín Glas Bán locked up
Sarah in the harness room.

The prince's share had hardly sunk into the sod when
it hit a rock and broke. He was afraid to go back and look
for another plough, so he sat by the fence and wept. After
lunch, An Pilibín Glas Bán again read and took a nap.
Sarah called a servant and asked for a drink of water. As
soon as she got it, she turned herself into a tadpole, spilled
the water on the ground and swam out under the harness
room door to a stream that flowed past the *bánóg*. There
she changed herself back into human form.

'You're not doing too well,' she smiled.

'Indeed and I'm not,' answered the prince.

'Here, give me the reins.' Sarah urged the horses on
and, even with the broken share, she turned the straightest
furrow the prince had ever seen. In less time than it takes
to tell, she ploughed and harrowed the field. Then she
told the prince to bring the animals back to the stable
yard. He did so and An Pilibín Glas Bán emerged, fresh
after his rest. When the prince told him that the work was
completed, he did not believe him. But he flew up into

the air and saw for himself. As he re-alighted he gave the
prince his third and hardest task.

'You see that castle on the hill that rises above the
wood?' he asked.

'I do,' answered the prince.

'There is a hen in its highest turret who has sat on a
clutch of eggs for four hundred years. Tomorrow you must
go there and fetch me both the hen and the nest of eggs. If
you don't, or if you break even one egg, I will behead you
with this sword,' he said, brandishing the weapon again.

Next morning the prince set off. He reached the
building and examined it. It had no door, window or
outer stairs. How was he to get to its highest turret?

Back, locked in the harness room, Sarah again
anticipated An Pilibín Glas Bán's rest period. She worked
the same ruse to get out and soon joined the prince at the
castle. She gave him a magic wand and told him to touch
her with it and then kill her. 'Cut me in two. Place one
set of my ribs against the wall and they will form stairs
halfway up. Then attach the other set of ribs and you will
have steps to the top.'

The prince cried more and protested. 'You have been
so good and kind and helpful. I cannot kill you.'

'If you don't, the two of us will be slain,' she said. 'Do
as I say, and when you are coming down the steps with the
hen and the eggs, touch each step with the wand and by
the time you reach the bottom, I will be restored.'

The prince did as she had instructed. Sarah's mutilated
sides brought him to the high turret where he grabbed the
hen and the eggs and ran back to descend. But when the
hen saw bright daylight after being so long indoors, it
pecked the prince's hand, making him forget to tip the
first couple of steps with the wand. When he remembered

and struck the fourth step, he, the hen and the nest
came tumbling down and Sarah stood before him.
Unfortunately, she was tilted to one side, being short three
ribs. Under her instructions, the prince again returned to
the green house and again An Pilibín Glas Bán emerged
after his rest. When he saw the hen and the eggs he was
dumbfounded.

'You surely are the best man that ever came this way,'
he smiled. 'You must marry my daughter, Sarah. I will
give you the castle and all the wealth you could wish for.'

That was the first time the prince realised that Sarah
was the bird's daughter. It was also the first time he did not
detect malice in the voice of his captor.

'I would love to marry Sarah, sir, but first I must go
back and tell my parents.'

'Go then, but make a solemn promise that you will
return.' There was affection in the voice of An Pilibín
Glas Bán.

That night there was feasting and dancing and when
the revelry ended, the prince held Sarah in his arms and
kissed her. She warned him that he was never to kiss
another until he returned. 'If you do, you will forget all
about me,' she said.

Next morning, the prince mounted his steed and
returned to Ireland. His mother saw him reining in and
ran out to kiss him. The poor woman was deeply hurt
when he refused. So too were his relatives and friends,
none of whom he dared even embrace. His pet dog,
however, jumped up on his chest and nuzzled his damp
mouth against the prince's. As soon as he did, the prince
forgot all about An Pilibín Glas Bán, the tasks and the
help he had received from Sarah. He lived happily with
his parents for a few weeks, until the King of Ireland

reminded him of the rich girl he had been courting
before he left.

'Left where? I never left this place.' The king did not
like the strange look in his son's eyes as he uttered those
words. But he held his counsel. He arranged a banquet,
intending to announce that the wedding would take place
the following day.

Far away, in the purple house in the wood at the end
of the world, Sarah sensed that something was wrong. She
seized the hen that had been hatching for four hundred
years and a lazy cock that was around the farmyard as long
as she could remember. Mounting her father's finest mare,
she galloped towards Ireland. She landed near Wexford
and asked for lodgings. When he heard how far she had
come, her kindly host threw a party. Sarah remained aloof,
but after midnight she asked for a few oats for her fowl.
She scattered these on the floor and the cock and hen
started picking at them. Suddenly, the cock pecked the
hen's neck.

'Why did you do that?' the hen scolded. 'Do you not
recall when I tossed out the hay and found my great-
grandmother's needle for you?'

They ate more oats and again the cock pecked the
hen on the neck.

'Why did you do that?' the hen scolded. 'Do you not
recall when I ploughed and harrowed the *bánóg* for you?'

Again the fowl ate and again the cock pecked the
hen's neck. Once more the hen chided.

'Why did you do that? Do you not recall when I
killed myself getting the hen and eggs from my father's
castle for you?'

At that moment the prince realised that he wanted to
marry somebody more precious than the rich girl of his

father's choice. He also remembered everything that the dog's kiss had obliterated from his mind: An Pilibín Glas Bán, his difficult tasks and the lovely Sarah. At that moment, too, the King of Ireland wondered why he had thrown a party for a strange girl. He was confused when he thought he saw a hen and a cock on the dance floor one moment, the cock biting the hen's neck, and they both disappearing the next.

To his son the prince, however, everything was clear. He looked around and saw Sarah smiling at him. A few oats trickled from her hand and the prince moved closer and gave her a gentle love bite on her fair neck.

The prince and Sarah married next day and the couple lived happily ever after.

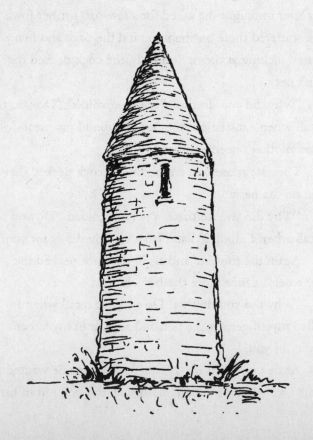

THIRTEEN

The Fear Dearg and the Princess

'There's a stepmother's bite in that day.' The Irish saying is as unkind to stepmothers as is its fairy lore. These women are always depicted as being cruel to the children they did not bear. One such person, a Carlow woman, had a daughter of her own when she became widowed and then married the King of Leinster. The girl's name was Gunóg. The king too had a daughter who bore no other name but Beanflaith, meaning princess. This girl was very beautiful and the stepmother became extremely jealous of her. She decided to send her on a hazardous errand and consulted a blind *saoi*, or wise man, who lived near the palace. On his advice, she dispatched Beanflaith to the Eastern World to find and bring back three bottles of healing water, *uisce sláinte*. She gave Beanflaith a small amount of food for her journey.

The girl had barely begun her journey when she met a Wicklow Fear Dearg. This is a small fairy who wears a red cap and cloak and can steal a baby from a crib and leave a changeling from his own people in its place. He can do good too, if treated kindly.

'Give me one of your juicy crubeens, gentle lady,' he asked.

'God knows, I don't have much, but what I have I will share with you, my wee man,' Beanflaith answered with a smile. They ate heartily and Beanflaith then stood to continue her journey. Before leaving, she told the Fear Dearg of her quest.

'Sit down out of that and listen to my advice,' ordered the fairy. Beanflaith obeyed and the man told her how her stepmother was acting out of ill-will. He also told her how to accomplish the task without being harmed. 'Just do whatever you are told by whomsoever you shall meet and you will be all right. Now, away with you *agus go n-éiri an bóthar leat*' (and may the road rise with you, i.e. safe journey).

When she reached the well and leaned over its parapet to fill the first bottle, a mighty dark man arose from beneath the water. 'Wash me and clean me and leave me back in the water,' he commanded. Although taken aback, Beanflaith remembered the Fear Dearg's advice and obeyed. A second dark man then arose and asked the same. She washed and cleaned him and left him back too. When she did the same with the third and fourth dark men, the bottom of the well turned to blood and the top, honey. Beanflaith filled her bottles and as she did, the four men came out of the water again. They conversed about how to reward her and one made her even more beautiful than before. The second gave her protection

against her enemies. The third told her that everything
she touched thereafter would taste like honey. 'And what
will you give this lovely girl as a present?' they asked the
fourth. 'I will give her this. She will have something
more every evening than she started the day with and
will have eternal happiness.'

Beanflaith returned home and handed the bottles
to her stepmother. When she saw the girl's increased
beauty and happy smile and when Beanflaith told her
what happened, the woman was furious. Off to the *saoi*
she went and gave him a tongue-lashing. 'Instead of
bringing her harm, you brought her good fortune,' she
chastised. The old man advised her then to send her
own daughter, Gunóg, on the same errand. 'Then she
will be the loveliest and luckiest woman in the world,'
he said.

She sent Gunóg off and she too met the Fear Dearg.
He asked for a crubeen but she refused, saying, 'Away out
of that, you wizened and warty creature. How dare you
approach a well-bred lady like me!'

She reached the well in the Eastern World and the
first black man popped up and asked her to wash him and
clean him.

'Me, a fine lady, wash the likes of you?' she screamed
in dismay. 'I will do no such thing.'

She told the same thing to the second, third and
fourth. When she uttered her last refusal, the bottom of
the well turned to honey and the top turned to blood.
Gunóg filled her bottles and left for Ireland, not knowing
that the four dark men had arisen from the well and were
casting curses on her. When her stepmother saw her, she
nearly fainted. Gunóg was uglier than before and she wore
a black scowl and talked in a cantankerous manner. There

was a horrible smell from her and anything she touched turned filthy. That night, the old *saoi* got the length and breadth of the stepmother's tongue. 'The girl is like a gaol door with the bolt pulled — useless!' she said.

During the following months, the stepmother grew more and more angry, while her daughter grew crosser and crosser. Everything she touched turned to powder and the king wondered why his palace was falling asunder.

Consumed with jealousy, the stepmother eventually put Beanflaith in a barrel, got her own family to help her roll it to Wexford and throw it over a cliff into the sea. Huge waves buffeted the barrel and Beanflaith was feeling sick when, all of a sudden, she felt herself rolling gently along some very soft surface. She pushed for all she was worth, prised the barrel open and gasped at what she saw. A bright sun shone down from a cloudless sky on lush green fields whose hedgerows sparkled with flowers of diamond and silver. A handsome young man with fair hair and blue eyes was smiling at her.

'I saw the barrel heading for the rocks and waded out to bring it here,' he said. The couple went to the young man's house and the family welcomed Beanflaith and invited her to stay with them. She did, and the couple fell in love and married. One year later, Beanflaith gave birth to a child.

She felt a little lonely for her own people, however, so she wrote to her stepmother asking for news of her father and members of the household. The stepmother told nobody of this, but took a magic wand given to her by the *sidhe* and set out to visit Beanflaith. Gunóg came too. When they landed, Beanflaith rushed to meet them, but instead of a kiss, the stepmother slapped her across the face with her wand, uttered a curse and Beanflaith was turned into a hare. She struck Gunóg with the wand too and, although it did not improve her appearance, the spell made Beanflaith's husband think Gunóg was his wife. The stepmother knew that Beanflaith, although now a hare, could converse with her husband after dark, so each night she gave the young man a potion that made him sleep through until dawn. Beanflaith came to his bedroom window each night and told her woeful tale, but he could not hear her.

Realising that she could not stay on the island for ever, the stepmother asked the young man to hunt a hare for her, saying Gunóg had creeping sciatica and needed soup made from a hare from a magic island to cure it. Neither the young man nor his family had ever heard of such a thing as a hare, let alone seen one, but the wicked woman described the animal to them and assured them that there was such a beast on the island.

So the young man set off to hunt the hare, not knowing that if he killed it, his lovely wife would be lost for ever. When Beanflaith saw him, she longed to run up and kiss him, but the protection given to her by the dark man of the well urged her on. The hunt continued for three days, and as the young man returned to his home on the third evening, who should he meet but the Fear Dearg that had advised Beanflaith in the first place. This little man told the young man all about Beanflaith's stepmother and her evil intentions. He said, 'The hare you hunt is your wife. The unfortunate girl comes to your window every night but cannot talk to you because you are in a deep sleep. Tonight, find some way to avoid drinking the potion.'

When he reached home and announced that he had not killed the hare, the stepmother said, 'Tomorrow you

will. Get to bed early and have a good sleep.' But when
she handed him the potion he pointed to the roof and
said, 'Isn't that a beautiful bird that has started building in
the thatch?' The woman looked up and as she did, the
young man spilled the drink on to the fire. There was a
loud explosion and a purple flame leaped up the chimney.
When the woman recovered her composure, the young
man was rubbing his lips, saying, 'That is truly the nicest
drink I ever had.' He rubbed his eyes and went to bed,
feigning heavy snoring within minutes. When the
stepmother heard this, she smiled and went to her own
bed, contented.

Beanflaith, still a hare, came to the bedroom and
spoke words of love to her husband. He promised to
release her from the spell the next day. At dawn, he arose
and crept into the room where Gunóg and her mother
slept. He took the woman's magic wand from under the
bed and touched her and her daughter with it. Both of
them turned into rock and rolled from the bed, out the
door and into the field behind the house. But for the spell
of protection from the first dark man of the well, the
stones would have crushed Beanflaith, now returned to
her human state and running to fall into the arms of her
beloved husband.

FOURTEEN

The Seven Year Son

A County Clare farmer's daughter became pregnant by the son of a king of Thomond. His queen was in league with the fairies, who advised her to pick certain herbs and hang them from the ceiling in her kitchen. They said that no child would be born to the farmer's daughter while they hung there. The farmer did not know about this and he wondered why his daughter had morning sickness every day for seven years. He was destitute from paying priests, doctors and all sorts of quacks and faith healers. Some of them told the farmer his daughter was pregnant, but he would not believe them, naturally, because no confinement ever lasted that long.

A traveller called at the farmer's house one day. He had not called there for some years and so he noticed the decline in the property. 'What happened to make you so down and out?' he asked. The farmer told him the whole story and the traveller offered to have a look at the girl. He too confirmed the girl's condition but he told the farmer he would try to help. Off he went to the royal kitchen, hoping to sell some goods to the king's household. He took out besoms and sleans for display and while the staff examined these he looked around and saw the herb-bag, now dirty and black, hanging from the rafters. As he gathered up his things, he deliberately swung the slean high and cut it down. At that very moment the farmer's daughter gave birth to a boy. Because of his delayed arrival, they called him Seven Year Son.

He grew into a strong lad, because the *sidhe* had nourished him while in his mother's womb. At 15 years of

age he stopped the king's coach and four in full gallop by
hanging out of it. Then he jumped in and asked the king
for his daughter's hand in marriage. The king told him he
would have to undergo some tests to prove himself worthy.

The first was to go over to England and make his
brother, the King of England, laugh three times. Each
chuckle would have to be loud enough to be heard in
Clare. Seven Year Son crossed the sea and met the king,
but it is hard to amuse English royalty. Even though he
drank with him all night and told every story he could
muster, there was no laugh out of the monarch. Next day
the king told him to look after his cattle and to follow
them as far as they went grazing. They came to a patch of
hungry grass, a fairy trap for mortals. Seven Year Son
stepped on it and a large wall appeared before him. He
battered his head against it and made an entrance for the
cattle. Inside was an orchard where an abundance of huge
red apples hung from the trees. The trees were high, so the
lad climbed one and began eating the fruit.

A giant came along and picked up one of the cows
and stuck it under his arm. He was walking away with it
when Seven Year Son called after him, saying it belonged
to the king. The giant was furious, so he flung the beast
into the tree. The Irish king's son caught it by a horn and
climbed down the tree with it. He left it with the others
and although only up to his knees, he began wrestling
with the giant. In no time at all he had the giant
screaming for mercy. In return for mercy, he offered the
lad a lamp that would light the world. Seven Year Son
took it, then made a swipe at the giant's poll with it. The
blow took the head clean off at the neck. It went
bouncing around the orchard and the lad chased and
kicked it. The head kept abusing the lad, when who

should come by but the King of England and he let out a laugh that was clearly heard in Clare.

The king was even happier next morning when his herd yielded more milk than the palace had vessels to hold. He sent Seven Year Son off with the cows again and the same thing happened when they came to the hungry grass. When the boy was gorging himself in the tree, a double-headed giant loomed up. They threw insults at each other and again this led to wrestling and the giant's pleas for mercy. He said, 'I will give you the Sword of Strength if you release me. You are the strongest man I ever met, but this will make you the divil entirely.' The lad took the sword and sliced the two heads off the giant with it. They hopped around the trees and the boy chased them shouting that this was the best game of football he ever had. The heads kept hurling abuse and the King of England passed by and laughed louder than before. This time, people in Aran as well as Clare heard it.

When the King of Ireland heard the guffaw, he was amazed. A little worried too, and wondering what a wedding would cost him, because the farmer's son was now two-thirds of the way towards winning his daughter's hand. Things were becoming even more complicated because, unknown to her father, the King of England's daughter had her eye on Seven Year Son. His feats of strength and good looks impressed her.

Next day, the lad set off again with the king's cattle. Things happened as before, only this time the giant that appeared had three heads. He really abused Seven Year Son. 'You're nothing but a low-down Irish coward. You picked on my young brothers yesterday and the day before. They were only 100 and 200 years old — scarcely out of the crib.'

'About time they thought of getting out of the envelope,' quipped the Irish lad, jumping down and beginning to wrestle.

This time, when the giant was appealing for mercy, he offered Seven Year Son the keys of a silver castle that suddenly appeared, as castles tend to do in fairy stories. 'Inside there is all the wealth you could wish for and, what's more, I will become your butler,' he promised.

Seven Year Son took the keys but scolded, 'If I need a butler, he won't be an ugly-looking gazebo with three heads and not a whit of manners in him.' With that, he drew the Sword of Strength and chopped the three heads off as if they were ears of corn. He began playing football with them, dribbling and hopping one against the other. When he kicked the three of them in the air at once, the King of England arrived and let out the most enormous laugh ever heard in that country before or since. The King of Ireland heard it and realised that he should send out the wedding invitations.

Seven Year Son knew he had completed his work, but he decided to have a look about the silver castle before he returned to Ireland. In its kitchen an old man and woman sat on either side of the hearth. A big black cat lay between them.

'You're the Irishman what killed my three sons,' said the old man.

'That's him,' the woman added.

'None other,' mewed the cat.

'You won't leave this castle until you fight me,' the old man shouted, jumping to his feet.

'And me.' The woman was on her feet too.

'Not to mention me,' squealed the cat.

The woman attacked first. She had steel spurs on her fingers for all the world like a fighting cock's. She scraped and tore at the lad's face and throat, but in the end he got the better of her and killed her.

On his hands, the old man wore rings with small blades welded into them. He raised these, but Seven Year Son sliced off his head before he could come within range.

When the cat stood up, a few tons of ashes dropped to the floor. Some of it went into the lad's eyes, blinding him temporarily. The cat stuck its tail into the fire and lit its tip. It scorched the eyes and ears of Seven Year Son. The fur stopped burning but not before it exposed an iron gaff. The cat whirled around the kitchen, describing an arc with its tail. This split Seven Year Son open from belly to neck.

Meanwhile, the daughter of the King of England was looking for him everywhere. When she came to the castle and saw the door open, she entered and came across the carnage. She wailed and keened and clung to the remains of Seven Year Son. One scream made the cat leap on to the mantelpiece with the fright. Noticing the movement, she looked up. There was a bottle beside the cat. She took it down and read its label:

Prescribed by the fear leighis of the sidhe. Can cure carbuncle and palsy in goats or humans. Can cure death itself if rubbed all over within an hour of demise.

Potion of a fairy doctor! Not believing her luck, she massaged the lad with the oil. His gaping wounds snapped closed and he hopped to his feet. From the mantelpiece, the cat said, 'This time I will kill you and the girl so that you won't rise a second time.'

'There are no ashes on your back to help you now,' shouted Seven Year Son, grabbing the Sword of Strength

and holding it at the ready. When the cat tried the trick
with its tail, Seven Year Son caught it in mid air and sliced
it up.

The daughter of the King of England ran to his arms
and kissed him. Then she led him through all the rooms in
the castle and each was a different country. Oriental glades
gave way to sea-washed stretches of sand. Western skies
blended with magical northern lights and southern stars.
There were snow-covered hills, blazing sun and pasture.
The lad was enchanted at such beauty and the girl took
advantage of this.

'Couldn't you live here with me instead of returning
to Ireland? Am I not as attractive as the daughter of your
own country's king?'

Seven Year Son said he did not wish to offend, but he
explained that he had given his word and must return. He
gave the girl the keys, however, and told her to enjoy the
wealth that they would bring. 'I have all I could wish for
back home,' he added, 'and, never fear, you will find a
man nearly as good as me sometime.' Even his vanity did
not put her off, but she knew she would have to be
resigned to losing him.

Well, that night, the king brought Seven Year Son to
dinner in the palace. While they were eating, a stag
appeared at the window. Seven Year Son almost retched
when he saw what happened. The king opened the
window and allowed the stag to defecate into his mouth.
Appalled and disgusted, the Irish lad jumped to his feet
and swore to kill the rude animal. The king said, 'Do no
such thing. That stag comes here only when I have guests.
It wishes to bring shame on me. But if you do not go
home quickly, God knows what might happen to you.
Seven years ago a stranger came here and asked for my

daughter's hand. At supper, he reacted just like you. Next day, he and my two sons went hunting the stag. I have never seen them since.'

At breakfast, next morning, the stag came to the window again and the same disgusting procedure followed. It was too much for a clean-living Irish lad, so Seven Year Son left his royal fry and took off after the animal. The deer kept the same distance between them, but just as it was nearing its den, the Irish lad sprang through the air and landed near enough to draw blood with a swipe of his sword. The stag hobbled on and Seven Year Son followed it into a dark cave. When his eyes got used to the light, he saw a butcher carving up a live *banbh*. The poor young pig was squealing, so he had to shout to be heard.

'Did you see a dirty stag come in?'

'The only thing dirty I saw was yourself,' answered the butcher.

'Don't be so smart! Did you see anything come in?'

'Only yourself.'

'Well then, you must be the stag,' Seven Year Son shouted, as he lifted the butcher's apron. Sure enough, blood was dripping from his flank. 'Now, where are the three men who hunted you seven years ago?'

'They are upstairs, turned into stone. And if you cannot prove your manliness, you will become an ornamental pebble yourself,' said the stag.

'What proof do you want?'

'When this *banbh* is boiled, you must take him out of the pot with just the fork.'

That was no trouble to Seven Year Son. He lifted the pig, pot, crane and all with one hand. He then ordered the stag to go upstairs and return the men to their proper shapes. It did so and the boy told them to go back to the palace and be good to their father and sister. Then he turned to the stag, now restored to animal form. 'I will give you one chance. Go to the king's palace in the morning. I will follow you. If I do not catch you, you will be safe. If I do, you will die.'

Next morning the stag did indeed set off for the palace. Seven Year Son followed but, like before, could not gain any ground on it. As a result, the stag was already acting as before at the window when Seven Year Son caught up. He cut the head clean off the dirty creature. The king was delighted; more so when Seven Year Son told him that his two sons and prospective son-in-law were even then on their way home.

It took the others seven days — testimony to the agility of Seven Year Son. There was great jubilation and Seven Year Son waited until the suitor wed the King of England's daughter. Then he returned to Ireland and had another great day when he married the daughter of the King of Ireland. The couple, their parents, the English king, his daughter and her husband lived happily ever after. That makes seven!

FIFTEEN

A Cork Banshee

I n times past, if a child found a rack or comb with broken teeth in a hedgerow, it brought anxiety to the heart. Terror, sometimes, because such an implement was, sure as God, a *cíor bean chaoint*, a keening woman's comb. In other words, it belonged to the *Morrígan*, the *badb* or, more commonly, the Banshee. This fairy woman followed certain families, mainly Gradys, Kavanaghs, O'Neills, O'Donnells and O'Briens. On the night before the member of a household died, she howled in the distance, the terrifying cry coming nearer as the moment of death approached.

A well-to-do Cork widower called Grady had one son, Henry, and three daughters, Angela, the youngest, Mary and Julie. When Grady died, his son joined the army, so his brother managed his estate and kept the girls in luxury. Privately taught, their music teacher was a violinist. This man, George Freeman, was of noble descent, but was a man-about-town and a compulsive gambler. He was forced to give lessons to repay some of his gambling debts. He infatuated the three girls with his superb music. Being the eldest, Julie felt she had the true right to become his beloved. This aroused the jealousy of Angela, who considered herself madly in love with the man.

Twenty-year-old Julie was a sleep-walker, and her father had devised numerous methods of keeping the mansion safe and of ensuring that his eldest daughter never left the house when asleep. For one thing, he had Mary share her bedroom and he tied the clothes of Julie's bed to

hers, so that she would be alerted to any movement. The
jealousy between Julie and Angela was developing into
enmity when Mary went on holiday to Scotland.
Consequently, when her father asked Angela to take
Mary's place in Julie's bedroom, she begged to be excused.
Being a doting father, he agreed.

The girls' governess, Beth, was reading to Angela one
June evening. A red sun was sinking over the woodland
that surrounded the estate, painting the manor lake red.
Angela thought it a glorious sight, but the feeling of well-
being it brought faded when Beth began to confide in her.

'You know, child, that the Banshee follows the
Gradys. She wailed around this house before your dear
mother died and, as for the night before your father passed
away, God rest his soul, she was roaring like Doran's ass.'

Beth was inclined to scoff, but noticed the concern in
the old lady's eyes, and listened intently.

'I'm as worried as a clocking hen these two days past,
because on Monday night I heard the very same cry. Your
brother and sister are in foreign parts and who knows what
might have happened to them, God between us and all
harm.' Just then the postman arrived, bearing a letter from
Mary in which she told Angela about the great time she
was having. It helped to ease Angela's anxiety, but Beth's
information preyed on her mind all day, and when she
went to bed that night she prayed for her family as she
had never done before. She prayed and prayed and finally
dropped off to sleep.

Wakening a few hours later, she heard the village
clock striking two. The moon was casting a pale wash
through net curtains that were moving slightly in a gentle
breeze. So a floral outline moved along her counterpane
and across the floor. The design seemed to gather into the

shape of a woman and when the breeze lessened, it floated towards the window. A cloud then scurried across the moon and the shadow disappeared. Angela knew she should not be afraid, but something prompted her to get out of bed and look out. Just as she did, the cloud parted and the moon shone down on the woodland and lake. What Angela saw stuck her to the floor in terror. A woman was standing in her uncle's boat, her hands outstretched. She appeared like the outline Angela had seen in her room earlier, but was fully formed and clad in a white nightgown. It was Julie. She bent at the waist, untied the mooring rope and the boat began to leave the shore.

Throwing on a gown, cloak and shoes, Angela sped downstairs, out across the lawn, through the orchard and on towards the mooring platform. Another cloud crossed the moon and plunged the place into darkness. Angela tripped over an oak root and hit her head off the mighty trunk. She cried out in pain and thought she heard an answering wail from the woodland. It became louder and then changed into an evil cackle before dropping suddenly and becoming an almost soothing keen. Then the moon reappeared.

The boat was rocking gently a few yards from the shore. Its keel lay across Julie's waist. Weeds and sedge held her head and feet under the water, while her nightgown rose and dropped on the rippling surface. Angela gave a low moan of grief and fainted.

Meanwhile, George Freeman was up early and setting off for a morning's hunting. He was riding past the wood when he heard either the Banshee's cry or Angela's. He spurred his horse in that direction and soon came across the tragic sight. He carried Angela to the house and alerted the servants, who then attended to Julie's corpse. Mary Grady came home in time for the funeral but nobody could trace the whereabouts of Henry, who by that time had left the army.

Two years later, poor Beth was dead and Angela still loved George Freeman. He visited the house regularly but she never told him of her feelings.

Mary was reminiscing with her sister one evening. The two girls were laughing over some childhood memories when Mary jumped to her feet with a startled look on her face.

'That wailing, Angela. Do you hear it?'

'I hear nothing but the song of the thrush in the orchard,' Angela answered, and Mary fell back into her chair in a faint. When she recovered she told Angela that she had heard the Banshee's cry again. Although she did not admit it, Angela was terrified. Almost immediately, they heard hurried footsteps on the stairs. A servant knocked and entered.

'Mr Gray's footman is waiting below, Miss Mary. He has a coach and four outside and says his master is expecting you and Miss Angela.'

The girls could not understand this. They had never met Mr Gray, who had arrived in the locality from England during the past year. Neighbours had reported that he was quiet and retiring and was in ill-health. They questioned the footman as to the reason for the request, but he could only say that his master had said it was a matter of great urgency. Both ladies dressed and went to Mr Gray's home. The footman brought them upstairs to his master's bedroom. A grave-faced doctor stood by the bed in which lay a wasted, sickly man. Only when he spoke did the ladies realise that this Mr Gray was their brother Henry. In barely audible words, he told them of his years in the army, where he was penniless, and out of it, when he accumulated great wealth. Mary and Angela wept when he said that he missed his home terribly but was afraid that nobody would forgive him or allow him to enter his old home. 'So I bought this house, left the 'd' out of my surname and posed as Mr Gray. All the time, I watched my dear sisters from afar. I prayed for their welfare.'

He smiled weakly, then lay back and died. A will disclosed that he left all his wealth to Mary and Angela.

The Banshee had heralded the death of another
Grady. Angela was disturbed and miserable. More so the
following year, when George Freeman married Mary
Grady. Angela never revealed her love for him. She
remained single for life.

Sixteen

The Ball in Donegal

Twenty years old and single, Manus McGilligan was searching for a lost ewe in Donegal's Bluestack Mountains one day. He did not realise how late in the evening it was until the sun sank and he was left in darkness. Unable to find his way home, he lay down under a lone bush on a mossy ridge. It was a fairy thorn. He fell asleep, but almost immediately a well-dressed, handsome man awakened him and invited him to a ball which Lord Barnes Mór was giving. Manus had never heard of such a man but, being a lively lad and game for diversion, he agreed immediately. The gentleman walked him through sweet-smelling fields of flowers and fruit. Birds with multicoloured plumage sang in the trees. They passed by streams where silver salmon leaped and glistened in the warm glow of a golden sunset. Manus felt at peace.

His escort led him up a red-gravelled avenue to a large
blue castle, the biggest building Manus had ever seen. It
had fifty chimneys and a hundred windows and each of its
ten doors was as high as Errigal Mountain. A footman
opened the widest of these and they entered. Servants in
braided livery rushed hither and thither, bearing salvers of
viands. One noticed the couple arriving. He came over
and bowed, smiled to Manus's escort and led the way up
an ivory staircase.

'Meet Lord Barnes Mór. My lord, this is Mister
Manus McGilligan.' The young man made the
introductions.

'Welcome to my castle!' the tall man said. 'Pray, join
in the feasting and dancing.'

Manus became embarrassed. 'I'm not in my blue
Sunday suit, sir. How could I join all these fine people
dressed up like bushes at holy wells,' he said. Lord Barnes
Mór smiled and told a servant to bring Manus away to his
own room and dress him appropriately.

The walls of the lord's room were lined with ebony-
framed mirrors. Crystal chandeliers hung from a gilt roof,
surely a hundred of them, because the room was two miles
long. Footmen came to attend Manus. They tried on
green suits, blue cloaks, yellow waistcoats and white
knickerbockers, but he spotted a crimson costume with
lace trimmings and said he liked it. He put it on and felt
very self-confident. A bell rang and a butler directed him
to the ballroom. Such opulence he never could have
imagined, let alone witness, back in his hillside townland.
As he descended a flight of marble steps his escort
announced, 'My lords, dukes, barons, ladies and other
folk, allow me to present to you Mister Manus McGilligan
who will honour you with his company for the evening.'

Everybody bowed and Manus felt very important altogether.

Then all the beautiful ladies in magnificent dresses looked his way and he winked at two of them. They rushed over to him and began fighting about who would dance with him. As they argued, another young lady took his arm and began to waltz. Never had he heard such lovely music, although there were no musicians. It seemed to come from beneath the floor. Also, he realised that, although he had never danced anything but a reel or a jig, he was waltzing better than the most elegant gentleman on the floor. The night went on and one lovely lady after another asked him to dance.

The men began to get jealous and one tried to trip Manus during a minuet. His partner chastised him and asked Manus for the next dance. She told the other women what had happened and they all left their menfolk and lined up waiting their turn for a dance with Manus. He did polkas and quadrilles to beat the band (even though there was none). Such grace and litheness were never seen. The attention and the exertion were too much, however, and before half the line of applicants received dances, Manus collapsed.

'I'm exhausted, ladies,' he apologised. He looked out the door of the ballroom and saw servants with piles of roast quail passing by. Only then did he realise that he had not eaten since breakfast and that he was ravenous. He winked at the women and said, 'Maybe now if you gave me something to eat, I might recover some of my strength and give a few more of you a whirl.'

'Oh yes! Oh yes!' called the ladies. 'Give him some quail.'

'Oh no! Oh no!' called Lord Barnes Mór. 'We must have a tale.' He turned to the ladies. 'Shame on you. You all know the rules of this castle.' Then he explained to Manus that before he ate he must tell the assembled company a story.

'A story!' laughed Manus. 'I never told a story in my life. I have no stories.'

Lord Barnes Mór frowned. 'No story? What sort of an Irishman are you that cannot make up a story? Well, I'm afraid I have bad news for you, my lad. No tale, no quail. We here frown on people who cannot amuse us with a saga or two. And I might add that we think such a numbskull is useless to man, beast or bullock. I'm afraid you will have to leave us.' With that, the servant who had attended to him all evening placed his little finger under Manus's knee and tossed him out the window as if he were a feather.

Downhearted and alone, Manus made his way down the red avenue. At its gate he came across three undertakers who were trying without much success to lift a coffin. 'We need a fourth man under the tail and here's the very fellow. Slap your shoulder under this, Manus, for you know it is one of the works of mercy to bury the dead.' Manus obliged and soon they reached a cemetery. They put down the coffin and told Manus to dig a grave. He thought this a bit unfair but, although still very tired and hungry, he cut the sod and dug one. When it was ready, they began to lower the coffin, but a voice called from below. 'Shame on you for disturbing my poor father's skeleton. Fill up this hole immediately and bury your dead somewhere else.'

Manus said he was sorry, filled up the hole and dug another a few feet away. Again, when he had finished, he heard the voice. 'Shame on you for disturbing my poor sister's skeleton. Fill up this hole immediately and bury your dead somewhere else.'

By the time he had completed the third grave, Manus was in a state of utter exhaustion. He and the three undertakers began to lower the coffin, but the voice called again. 'Shame on you for disturbing my poor mother's skeleton. Fill up this hole immediately and bury your dead somewhere else.'

Well, the owner of the voice must have had a large extended family, for Manus dug grave after grave and was derided for disturbing skeletons of brothers, cousins, aunts, uncles, grandparents, godparents and half-sisters twice removed. His hands were peeling and the raw flesh pained him intensely. He buckled at the knees and his back ached. Perspiration rolled off him until the undertakers had to bale out every grave with a bucket.

Then Manus had an idea. He dug a grave five feet six inches, half a foot less than the others. He was hoping that the owner of the voice had no midgets in the family as he and the others lowered the coffin. He held his breath and waited for the voice, but none came. Lowering the remains, he was so relieved that he let the rope slide through his hands too quickly. The coffin hit the edge of the grave at an angle and the lid popped off. Manus looked inside and screamed. It was the corpse of Manus McGilligan.

'I knew I was dead tired, but this is the dickens entirely,' he screamed, before taking to his heels like a scalded cat. The three undertakers followed him and dragged him back. Despite his fatigue, he struggled and fought for an hour and a minute and began to get the

better of the others. Then he saw one of them draw a fairy
wand from under his cloak. As fast as a happy dog's tail he
weaved and ducked and snatched the rod. Then he tapped
each man with it and one by one they dropped dead.

Away with Manus to the castle then. The servant
who had attended to him when he arrived first was at the
door. He took Manus to the bathroom. Three young
girls washed him from head to foot. Manus was
embarrassed, but he felt refreshed and not at all tired.
Back to Lord Barnes Mór's room then for more fittings.
Footmen dressed him in an outfit even more elegant
than before. This time they carried him to the ballroom
in a golden sedan-chair that was upholstered in satin and
decorated with rare gems and trinkets. Everybody was
dancing as spiritedly as if the ball were only beginning.
One by one the ladies noticed him and three by three
they left their menfolk and surged forward to meet him.
But Lord Barnes Mór halted them and confronted
Manus.

'You said you had no story to tell. Why then should
you dare return?'

'Will you sit down there, your lordship, and not be
getting your periwig in knots. I have a story to unfold, the
like of which you wouldn't hear in a month of Sundays
and half an hour.'

'Very well then, take the throne.'

So Manus McGilligan sat on the fairy throne and
began his story. No *seanchaí*, no orator, no bishop, pastor,
abbot or politician ever received such attention. Men held
their breaths and women their hearts as words tumbled
from Manus like waters from a cataract. At the end there
was a moment of absolute silence, then a deafening
clamour. It rattled windows and doors until crows in

rookeries ten miles away awoke and gannets in the Saltee Islands thought there was another fair in Wexford. The fairy host clapped and cheered and Lord Barnes Mór came to Manus, shook his hand and said, 'I know I am only 1,000 years old, but never before have I heard such a mighty tale. And if I live another millenium, I know I will never hear the likes again.' Then he turned to the servants and said, 'Tend to this man as if he were the King of Ireland, the King of Spain and the King of France all wrapped up together. Nothing that we can provide is too good for him.'

Before the servants could respond, the women surrounded Manus and carried him shoulder-high to the banqueting room. They fed him the choicest sections of quail and other dishes and filled his glass repeatedly with the oldest and most expensive wine. When he could eat no more they carried him to a bedroom. They placed him on a bed dressed in gold-trimmed silk brocade. It was softer than anything he had ever felt before. One lady entered with a harp. She played the most exquisite music and in no time at all Manus fell asleep.

He awoke, but instead of looking into the eyes of a fairy harpist he was peering into the pupils of his lost ewe. The sun was shining down from above Barnesmore gap (Manus thought that name had a familiar ring to it). Then he remembered all that had happened. He was a little sad when he realised that he would enjoy no more of the high life that the Donegal fairies had given him. But he shook himself, stood up and began to guide the lost ewe back to his farm. In the farmyard he saw his spade where he had left it. Its handle was covered with blood and tiny pieces of flesh. Manus shook his head in wonder. He decided that life was good after all.

I'll never have to buy another drink as long as I have this story to tell, he said to himself. And he never did—until he moved south to Sligo, where they do not appreciate good storytelling!